Final Draft

Final Draft

Peter Hansen

Library of Congress Control Number: 2007902174
ISBN: Hardcover   978-1-4257-8538-3
                 Softcover   978-1-4257-8536-9
                 eBook   978-1-7960-2181-3

Print information available on the last page.

Rev. date: 08/26/2019

To order additional copies of this book, contact:
Xlibris
1-888-795-4274
www.Xlibris.com
Orders@Xlibris.com
575782

Part One

I get most of my story ideas at night, during a sort of purgatory between being awake and asleep; I have an odd sleeping disorder, so the ideas might come from dreams, might not. In any case, when fully convinced that I am awake, I scramble out of the sheets and write the idea(s) down on a little tablet I keep next to the bed. This is the same tablet I list words I'd like to use in my next story, collected from whatever novel I'd been reading the night before. (Current list: featureless, acerbic, epitaph, putrid.)

Some of the ideas seem brilliant at first, but the euphoria often dissipates when I try to put it to some worthy use. For instance, one morning I awoke with the story of an entrepreneur (me, written first person) who made millions inventing and manufacturing dildo telephones, novelty handheld telephones in various shapes and sizes of penises.

Now this *did* come in a dream, a very odd one involving the actor Michael Douglas wearing a pink bathrobe, and conducting a mail-order business out of my post office box. I was angry with him for collecting checks, maybe doing something shady, until I saw how much money he was making selling the dick phones. I thought of it as a hilarious farce. Picture this banner across the front of the book: "The true story of the miraculous *rise* (see the possibilities?) of Dickphone.com," or something like that. I even wrote a few pages of the novel, double entendres *spurting* out of me like—well, you get the picture. But after a few days it all became *flaccid*, and I went on to something else.

Others are truly wonderful ideas from the get-go (even if I am perennially unsatisfied with the written result), confirmed by unbiased friends with no ulterior objectives in the matter except to see their long-suffering starving artist friend finally reap some rewards for years of dedication to his art. These being financial rewards, of course. As in, "You finally might *sell* something!"

This is the story about two of those ideas for screenplays, one of which I presented for editing to a couple of (soon to be ex-) friends, the other an idea fortuitously birthed from the decision to do just that. Maybe that's the wrong word. This *birthing* was more mutant—the story yanked grotesquely from my guts like the creatures from the *Alien* films—than any sort of sweet maternal catharsis.

—

It took six exceedingly stressful months to write and rewrite the first script. I had to pass it like a kidney stone or it would kill me. It almost did anyway. Kidney stones and writers' ideas are very painful to purge. Those months were filled with the prescription slave-to-one's-art angst a *serious* artist must endure, or he cannot be, well, taken seriously. There were long sleepless nights facing the blur of the computer, and copious amounts of cigarettes, coffee, and alcohol, with pizza and pretzels whenever I needed nourishment. You get the picture. I kept the blinds drawn on the dangerous Southern California sun, notorious to me for its ability to fry an idea out of my brain like so much bacon. I'd head to the beach for the sun on my back, the heat burning through the permanently damaged muscles from too many hunched-over writing hours, the will to even care about *that* story gone forever.

Finally, one gray (thank God) June day, I emerged bleary-eyed from my Hollywood cave, my skin the color of the sky, and drove to the home of a colleague I'd met precariously years earlier at a writers' workshop at UCLA—while she was being forcibly removed. That afternoon she'd taken exception to a short story, which a Nordic-looking classmate had written, detailing the struggles an ex-Nazi soldier and his family had repairing their lives after the war. Linda was Jewish, and her grandparents had barely survived Dachau, so I guess she had every right to be touchy. But the story in question was really just a piece of crap, and the woman claimed she was only trying to show that there was suffering on all sides . . . blah, blah. Linda wouldn't have it. She tore at the poor woman during one of those touchy-feely discussions all writing workshops are known for, called her a skinhead, grabbed her hair, and nearly bopped her a couple times before I pulled her off—that's how we met. I sort of sided with her by saying something asinine like, "Maybe the parameters don't work here," or something equally ludicrous, which might have been interpreted by Linda to mean I agreed with her. In any case, as the rest of the class shook their heads at me, wondering what the fuck I was talking about, security was called, and a burly Samoan carried off Linda like a sack of potatoes. "Call me," she yelled back over the giant shoulder, reciting her number.

Linda Coen was ten years older than me and occasionally edited for spending money. She had a website, which really needed editing. She was also a struggling songwriter and artist. But she'd taken a different road than I to get to where she was (where we both were, at the time)—which was nowhere. She'd produced little in the way of real *work*, preferring to doodle junior-high-quality sketches—which mostly hung in her mother's house—and vacuous pop lyrics for one-hit wonders (okay . . . so she sold a of couple songs, she had to have *some* credibility for me to be marching over that script, didn't she?). She always had the financial support of wealthy parents back east, which allowed her to indulge in all kinds of LA goings-on. (Read: she'd been smoking dope, going to parties for decades, and I think was approaching a second face-lift). But now she was nearing fifty, her parents were retired, and they wanted to hang on to their dough. "Get a *real* job," they'd finally told her, twenty-seven years after she'd graduated from USC film school.

Linda was forced to move to the valley.

Into a Studio City studio, if that isn't redundant.

I could put this into a perspective befitting its significance, but I won't bore you with comparisons; there are so many. Okay, maybe a couple. Simply equate this with the exile of some ruler or the disgrace of some celebrity. Maybe picture Celine Dion in a hovel, down by the railroad tracks, sharing beans and franks with the homeless. That should do.

Anyway, Linda was also obsessive-compulsive—*maybe*. But before I go off cataloging her eccentricities in a manner you might consider rude, even cruel, allow my suspicions that her problem wasn't a true medical disorder, in which case I might or might not have had sympathy. No, I suspect she just chose to be eccentric, in that particular way so many in LA do—a geographic anomaly. The thing is, most of these people just fancy themselves artists. "I am a *serious* actor, a student of the craft." This is from people making their livings on soap operas, that sort of thing.

First thing I had to do was take off my shoes before I entered. Nope, sorry. First thing I had to do was slide a pan under my car's engine so I wouldn't drip oil onto her pristine cement guest parking space. (She'd had a special high-pressure wash done when she moved in.) The second thing I had to do was take my shoes off. Nope, sorry. I'll get it straight in a sec. The second thing I had to do was bang my feet against a special place along the railing of the stoop in front of her building. This was supposed to dislodge any dirt or pebbles attached to my shoes so that the hall of her place would remain as clean as possible. Now, I suspect Linda had tried, though not with me, to enact a policy of shoe removal at the front stoop. I imagined a wave of opposition not only from those who found the request preposterous, but also from others, more psychoanalytically prone, who might have suggested the feet in question would simply drag in said dirt on their stockings.

"Maybe even more," I could hear a soothing voice say. "The fabric on socks is often clingy." Lisa would have looked at the person with grave concern, then looked down at her new white carpet (why did people like this have *white* carpets?) and agreed.

"Oh yes," she would have gasped. "That would be *horrible.*"

These pre-door-knocking instructions had been mailed to me within a week after Linda moved, in a form letter suspiciously like those you get on Christmas from friends and relatives doing much better than you ever will. Her letter was richly detailed, with maps from wherever you were coming (north, south, east, west, up [Bob Hope Airport], down [Metro Subway]). There were two or three addendums involving neighbors to be wary of; animals not to pet on the way in (she was allergic to *all* animals); and, of course, ways to avoid dirt. There were seasonal footnotes too like steering clear of the aspens in the rear courtyard during the autumn so as not to track in dead leaves; and she'd heard they sprayed them with something in the spring so then was out too. However, so that we recipients of the letter would not think the move was a fall from grace, and in keeping with the holiday newsletter theme, pages 4 and 5 documented a year's embellished triumphs. Trips to New York, a story published in some now-defunct literary magazine, new boyfriend (already gone by the letter's publication), and so forth. The reason for moving was briefly mentioned as an attempt to downsize and "simplify" her life.

So there I was, obediently removing my shoes when the door flew open. And there she was, all mouth. She looked as if she hadn't eaten for days, weeks even.

"Hi!" she said. Had she been watching for me through the peephole? It wasn't as if there was going to be a newspaper sullying her doorstep.

"How'd you know I was out here?"

"Oh you. Silly." she said. That was her answer.

She pecked me on both cheeks with moist, dirigible lips. Had she had those done? Or were her proportions skewed, now that she was bulimic?

Inside I could hear Joni Mitchell's "Help Me (I Think I'm Falling)." I should have taken the cue right then and there. But all I could think of at the time was Joni Mitchell. Though stuff like that comes back to you, even the lyrics, you can sing them right off; it really had to have been thirty years since I'd heard that song. Uh-oh. Linda was in one of her hippie moods. This was when she'd wear ankle-length Indian dresses, chant before a sandstone Buddha in spindly yoga positions, burn incense in little cast bronze trinkets, brew hibiscus tea, and smoke her pot.

"Come in, and have some tea," she said like the witch to Hansel. "Just brewed." She stepped back into the room and twirled. It was more Stevie Nicks than a pirouette, more sensimilla than Tchaikovsky. I watched as she made her way to an old CD player to (hopefully) turn the volume down.

She turned the volume up.

Joni was now screaming, "Help me!"

"I'll be back in a minute," Linda said, rounding a corner.

I shrugged and stepped in. Cautiously. Though I had successfully undergone the decontamination process, I still felt, well, a little dirty. Maybe it was guilt about the empty candy wrappers on the floor of my car; maybe it was the exhaust from a bus, which gusted past me as I walked from the garage to the front stoop. Maybe it was all of the smog, or just LA in general. Whatever, I just didn't feel as if I measured up to her *sense of clean.* I looked at my fingernails as I entered her sanctuary. Maybe that was it. Nope. Clean. Oh well.

Linda had disappeared into the kitchen, I assumed. I'd been there once before. Off to one side in a cubbyhole, that's where the kitchen was. It was the only place she could have gone, the rest of the apartment being directly in front of me. Now, don't get me wrong; I'm not making snotty judgments about the size or glamour of somebody's home. Jesus, I lived in a shoebox at the time, across the hall from a crack dealer, next door to a pimp and his whore.

I'm just giving you a sense of how small this place was.

I looked around a bit at what there was to look at. She had the same living room set she'd had at her fancy digs in Palisades, though the overstuffed sofa set looked ridiculous here. It was some kind of rare Egyptian fabric; she'd given me the spiel once when I was pretending to listen but, of course, I'd forgotten what she'd said. She must have had to sell most everything else, though I wasn't going to ask. Maybe it was all in storage. What did I care? She'd probably start crying or something if I brought it up; she was weird about *things*. That's the way LA quasi-hippies are. They fancy themselves as spiritual, but they drive BMWs, get their hair and nails done by people like Jose Eber, take fancy trips to Cancun, step over the homeless in their Gucci loafers, and all the rest—you know the drill. They're basically full of it.

Linda had her crystals out too. Laid out on the coffee table like we were going to have a séance or chat with a Vulcan or whatever. There were about ten of them. Jesus. Probably they each had some separate purpose; maybe one aligned you with one star, the other with the moon. I didn't know. She had some pot on the table too. That's another thing about entertainment people. They still do drugs at practically any age. Now I know pot doesn't really count, but I've seen people in LA, at parties, old-time movie people easily seventy or even eighty freakin' years old, holding courtlike, surrounded by cling-ons, lining up coke and ecstasy and meth! Please.

"Honey?" Linda yelled. She had to really yell too, Joni being as loud as she was.

"What?' I yelled back. She'd never called me honey before. I figured it was something to do with the mystic thing. We were all brothers and sisters and, well, honeys—though I didn't quite get the connection. I guess I was a little dim from all those months writing. Writing doesn't prepare you for the real world; you're creating your own, and you're sort of used to being *there*; but I don't want to get off on a tangent here.

"Do you want honey in your tea?" she yelled.

Jesus. "Uh, sure," I said. I wished Joni would shut her own big freakin' mouth up right about then. These two women were driving me crazy, and I'd been there for, what? five minutes?

I tried to think of somebody else who'd help me edit the damn script. If I hadn't thought it was so good, if certain friends hadn't encouraged me that this was *positively* the one, I would have filed it with all the other scripts, songs, stories, articles, and novels (yes, novels!) in an overcrowded four-drawer filing cabinet in my closet. What was I doing with so much work that hadn't been published? Why wasn't I hitting the pavement, mailboxes, or the internet, trying to sell the stuff? Because I thought it was all garbage. Not throwaway garbage but the-early-writings-of type of garbage. Whereas the fantasy was that someday I would become a famous writer, and publishers and fans would clamor for my early works, which I'd triumphantly dig out; and everybody (including me, jumping on the ol' proverbial bandwagon) would see the raw but undeniable promise.

So here I was with the first mutual masterpiece. Many other writings had passed the friends' test, none had passed mine; I hoped that didn't put me in some symbiotic relationship with Linda's obsessive-compulsive thing—a version of perfection difficult to achieve. (Lets none of us overanalyze this part of the story, okay?) I couldn't think of anyone who'd do the deed for Linda's fee, which was zero. Well, not exactly zero, it was a barter thing involving my photo skills and her wanting new head shots, but it was certainly no cash up front. Which was what I had. No cash.

So I was stuck with Linda. But the deal didn't include Joni, so when the next song ended, I promptly ejected the CD and flipped through the ancient stack, neatly arranged alphabetically or by genre or chronologically, who knew.

"Hey! What happened with the stereo?" Linda chirped. I hurriedly picked something, which was hard considering what my options were: Dan Fogelberg, James Taylor, Phoebe Snow, and Bon Jovi. (Quick, for ten points, which artist does not belong in this grouping?)

"Just a minute," I said, fumbling with what appeared to be the entire library of Dan Fogelberg.

"I liked that," Linda said. The teapot began to whistle, and she joined in with a little ditty we all know and love.

"I'm a little teapot short and stout," she sang. Jesus. I frantically picked something.

Well, at least I could get some nostalgia out of the hair band, so I carefully placed the Bon Jovi CD on the player, making sure no rogue dust particles found their way inside during the two seconds I had the lid flipped up. Though Linda might have had some special molecule detector installed, which would betray me. Luckily, no alarm went off, and the music came back on.

"Here is my handle; here is my spout," Linda said, reappearing with two large mugs of tea, one red, one blue. She handed me the blue one, a photo mug from about 1970, with a picture of a kitten dangling from a limb. "Hang in There Baby," it said. It was identical to a poster I'd received one Christmas when I was in elementary school. I didn't read Linda's mug; I could see it was about as ancient and depressing as mine so I avoided it, even tried looking away when it came near me.

Which it did almost immediately when we sat down on her white sofa. Linda scooted up all cozy next to me as if we were lovers at some ski lodge or something, drinking our hot-buttered rums, and playing footsie. She set that freakin' mug right in front of me, daring me to read it. Okay. Okay. I read the thing! Sometimes you've just got to do these things, get past them, and move on. There was a photo of two otters lying on their backs on some river or lake or something. The caption read, "You otter know I love you."

And Linda *did* lift her feet off the floor and tuck them under my leg (almost my thigh, just an inch or two shy). Though in fairness, that could have been the obsessive thing again; but how would that explain the tucking? And wouldn't her feet be just about as clean as the Immaculate Conception anyway?

But I let it all go, figured the whole thing was a small price to pay for a good edit, which I did trust her to do; and besides, I could always use this for writing fodder. I even began to console myself right then with that thought and looked hard at Linda for evidence of a multidimensional protagonist, which of course she was and then some. Satisfied and with a sly smile, evidently, I reached for the script, still snug under my arm.

"What are you smiling at?" Linda said. "You look like a little boy who's been out behind the woodshed." Whatever that meant.

"Oh, just thinking," I said, handing over the script. She took it, glanced at the title, and then set it on the table.

"Let's talk first," she said, gulping her tea in big, heavy swigs as though she was a disaster victim with her first soup in days. Her arms were like broom handles.

I'd been afraid she'd want to do the talk thing. It had always been fifty-fifty with her. Sometimes I'd begin to speak—it might even be at hello—while I'm still standing shoeless at the door, and she'd place a finger to my lips like my mother used to do in church.

"Peace," she'd whisper. "No words today. Let's just feed off each other's energy." Most of the time I thought her loony for that, those visits lasting about two or three minutes of unsuccessful telepathy before I'd bolt. But I'd wished for that now.

"Okay," I said. She shoved her feet deeper under my leg. I could feel her nails, for God's sake.

"Well," she said. "Tell me how you are. Besides the book I mean."

"Script."

"Besides the script then." Gulp.

So we spent the next hour or so going over in excess the details of my love life, family life, financial life, and other matters I never discussed with anybody, but which I indulged her in because, well, she seemed to need to be nurturing or something. Or she was stalling or she was nosy, I didn't fucking know. Anyway, since very little was happening in any of those areas, it was relatively easy for me to bring the discussion to a close before I put my fist through a wall. During the talk, she'd gotten up at least twice for more tea, to my single cup; and now she was frequenting the bathroom—which was connected to the living room, not even the humility of a cubbyhole. Which meant I could hear her pissing each time through a wafer-thin door. Voluminous torrents of urine in loud cascading waterfalls. Jesus, why even shut the door? Oh, and she was singing. The same Joni Mitchell song, which had played as I arrived. She sang when she pissed. Loudly. Louder than Bon Jovi, still on the stereo. I sat through three or four of these episodes before she finally returned to the sofa all peed out and picked up the script. I was thankful when she reached for her reading glasses on the coffee table, and we got down to business.

—

You will probably recognize the screenplay as this story progresses; that's the point here, unless you've been hiking the Gobi or something similar for the past few years. Because this is the *truth* behind the origins of the blockbuster film *Dr. Grim* (which started its life with the title below—more on that later), which became one of the highest-grossing films in history. I was the creator of the now-legendary alien doctor, sent to earth to rid the human race of the seven deadly sins. With his position as a kindly neighborhood general physician who always smiled (hence, the original title), he was able to inject thousands of unknowing patients with a serum he claimed was a vitamin injection. Everybody who took the serum passed the effects on to whomever they exchanged fluids with (kind of an anti-AIDS), as well as their children. Within a decade, an entire race of *nice* people inhabited much of the Western United States. The problem was, humans without the virus were bullying these people. The good people were weak, silly milquetoasts. Almost like Stepford wives or the inhabitants of Pleasantville. They couldn't function in the real world; they were unemployable, defenseless. They excelled at nothing. They needed the *evil* back. So the doctor, regrettably, had to find an antidote before things really got out of control. But, by the time he realized the severity, the times were reverting rapidly to a kind of Roman decadence, with entire populations of slaves and prisoners. Sacrificial sport was popular again; and the football stadiums were filled with thousands, cheering on the lions and tigers as they ripped at the flesh of the *good* race. It might have already been too late by the time Dr. Grin's antidote arrived from space. But you know what happened; you saw the movie, everyone did. And if you didn't, it's on DVD, go rent or stream it.

Dr. Grin

Screenplay by Peter Hansen

FADE IN:

1 INT. SUBURBAN DOCTOR'S OFFICE WAITING ROOM—DAY

CREDIT SEQUENCE. A receptionist answers a phone behind a desk. We hear a muffled voice. She is making an appointment for somebody. There are a few other people sitting around the room on nondescript sofas. A man flips through a magazine; a mother holds a child on her lap; and so forth.

———

We spent the entire day reading and rereading the script. Linda was fascinated, renouncing any additional high-maintenance behavior until hours later. Really, I'd never seen her just sit and do one thing, as long as I'd known her—which was over twelve years—so it was sobering to discover she could be (what is considered) normal.

Maybe that was the first sign—as I reflect with hindsight—that she was capable of maintaining an unexaggerated persona when it behooved her to be adult. I didn't catch it all then, like I should've; but my suspicions were increased that the baby-doll act was just that.

She even seemed a little matronly with the bifocals perched on the end of her nose; I might have been having tea with somebody's mother, for cryin' out loud. She turned the pages with a careful efficiency one would expect from any respected Hollywood editor, occasionally making little grunting noises when she approved or disapproved of some line, looking up a few times to say, even during the very first reading, "This is good, Peter; this is really good."

I was heartened, no matter how irritating she had been until then. After a marathon writing session, when you've regurgitated your guts in a lonely, martyristic exorcism as I had, it might not matter who endorses your work. Even so, I want to reemphasize that I had *some* respect for Linda, regardless of how thick I've been laying it on.

Eventually shadows fell across the room, and we both realized it was getting late.

Linda looked up from about her fourth reading. She'd finally made some minor marks on the script, a red slash here and there, nothing of substance.

"Let's call Robert," she said suddenly.

"Robert?" I asked. I should have known Robert would come up. Maybe I'd known even as I had called her a few days earlier. Linda could hardly take a breath without Robert. This was her self-described surrogate brother (occasionally incestuous? who knew?) whom she'd met at USC. They'd sludged through the LA muck together all these decades with surprisingly similar outcomes. Misery loves company, partners in crime, takes one to know one (my favorite). You pick the cliché.

—

Yes, Robert was himself entrenched in a dumpy shack just beyond Sunland, where the road starts to climb into the Angeles forest. I had last seen him at a party in Venice, where he tried to shrug off his misfortune by claiming he'd chosen the location because of its semi-rural flavor. Horses, wild hawks swooping about, hiking into the woods at the end of the day, the kaleidoscope of the sunset, all that crap. Please. I'd been to his neighborhood; another friend had languished there for a few months before giving up the grind and returning home to Indiana. You couldn't smell the forest for the meth labs; you couldn't hear the birds for the Harleys racing up the highway or the thousands of other vehicles heading for the hills, some carrying freshly mutilated bodies in their trunks to toss into some canyon. And many of the neighbors lived in dilapidated trailers, raised pit bulls, and held cockfights behind barbed-wired fortresses. On Sunday afternoons, enormous multiscarred and tattooed creatures collected money and watched for cops, herding salivating spectators toward their cinder block seats.

The sunset? A shit-brown pall in carcinogenic layers, the most lethal layer perpetually hovering around Robert's altitude—not to be confused with his attitude, which was his head up his ass, though the metaphor works both ways here.

Okay, so you get the picture, I might not have liked the guy. Besides the fact that he was a poorly disguised oil slick, here's the scoop on that:

Robert had been married once. I'd met the wife, nice girl (then anyway, ten years prior; she might have matured into a bitter Hollywood wannabe too, probably had, but I'm going off again here sorry). This was back when Robert was still in his late thirties, when there was still the—albeit *very* slim—chance he might make it in a town where you were old at thirty-five. It's worse for women, of course; but Robert, an actor then, was inching scarily close to character roles—the death knell for someone who'd always fancied himself as movie star material. This, by itself, was a joke; he'd have been lucky to get character parts. His fifteen years of relentless schmoozing, black-and-white glossies, and casting couches, had gotten him three commercials, a guest shot on a soap, one line in a cheesy TV movie, seven music videos—in which he could usually be seen doing a jerky little jig behind some long-forgotten band—and endless hundred-dollar days as an extra.

But he had this okay life, I guess, with the wife, their two adolescent daughters, the bit parts, which kept him optimistic, the semblance of youth. He still had his Hollywood dream; there was some *hope*. Linda introduced us at a poetry slam; and while we didn't exactly hit it off, we had this common friend, a mutual interest—Linda. I thought he was a smug, arrogant jerk; he thought I was a bleak gothic writer. I suppose we were both right. This was during the early days of my knowing her too, and I was fairly new to LA; and, if truth were really to be told, the whole thing (this seems indefinably absurd now, doesn't it?) enamored me, the idea that I was hobnobbing with people who were in the business. Jesus. Even if I was someone who still gave a shit, why hadn't I seen that these people were about as low on the food chain as you could get? We're talking bottom feeders. They don't even have names for those slimy mutant creatures creeping along the mud of my grandfather's pond back in Louisiana.

So we buddied around a few times—Linda, Robert, and I. We must have looked ridiculous. This was the 2000s, but Linda still worked the 80s leg warmer craze to new heights (or lows, depending on your perspective) and, literally, fashioned arm warmers, head warmers, hand warmers, knee warmers, whatever warmers. Robert sported one of those shag haircuts with an extra long (sometimes braided) tail you only see now on people of questionable birth, or on Hare Krishnas. Robert's wasn't just any ol' mullet though. His towered at least four inches on top (in a bizarre homage to the 50s rooster look) while that dastardly ducktail swung nearly to his ass. This was a guy who wondered why he wasn't getting roles. Who the hell was his agent?

And me? Everything was black, I even tried black eyeliner for a time. I was listening to too much Emo.

So there we were, the three of us. Robert's wife and kids always stayed home while we went to the showcases, the readings, coffee houses, and even the clubs sometimes. Don't worry, I won't spew any of that garbage like we were the three musketeers or some god-awful thing. Not even close. Like I said I didn't really even like Robert; I just hung around because I was an idiot. We were more like passing the time thinking LA was so cool, and we were so hot. There was always that day in the future when we'd hit it big; there was no doubt in our minds; it was just abstract as to when. Kind of like waiting for our fate, which we'd pluck out of the sky like a lost balloon. Sometimes there was this vague notion that we had to produce something to get there, but mostly we were biding our time. Linda would say something to Robert like "you better get something going" or "you have to get a job" and Robert would say "it'll come." Or Robert would ask Linda if so-and-so had called back about the demo, and Linda would say she wasn't worried about it. I noticed all of that but was falsely secure in my age difference. Anyway, the clock did keep ticking. Before long, the two of them turned forty; and they both freaked. There was one last incident before we stopped hanging out.

—

My sister had this great kid, Jeff. What a guy. I loved having this kid visit me; everything was always just perfect with him. He never complained, not once, when he'd visited me during those times. If I was busy or couldn't afford to take him to Universal or Disneyland or wherever the masses *have* to go if they visit Southern California, he'd make his own day just walking (in LA!) or take a bus to the beach, or go to a museum on his own. He'd cook hamburgers and Tater Tots and rent a video and have whatever piece-of-crap place I was living in looking all nice and homey when I'd return after a long day temping at some plastic surgeon's office or something. You think I'm just blowing this out my ass? You think there aren't people like this? Well, this kid was, and still is. He's the most selfless person I have *ever* met. Really, bear with me on the overkill; if you knew him, you'd understand. He was twelve when this all happened, so there was always the chance he was just pre-teenage cool, soon to evolve into the surly fuck every other teenager is. But he never did. As of this writing, years later, he's still my favorite person. He's in the Peace Corps now, can you freakin' believe that? I didn't even know there still was a Peace Corps! The kid's some kind of saint; he's in Niger or somewhere treating people with AIDS. He writes occasionally. I miss him. He never went through a month of being an asshole in his whole life.

Who knows why? My sister, she had the usual problems. Husband beat her; she drank, and she was sickly from living in the musty bayou all her life with mosquitoes so thick they drove the whole town batty. Lots of Southern Gothic secrets and all that. She died young, only forty-five, not too long ago. But her kid just rose out of that like the Resurrection.

Jeff's a looker too. Even at twelve, the little shit turned heads. Coal black eyes set deep in an olive face, straight black hair, kept just a little too long. He was already tall but not gangly then; his body grew in harmony, nothing sprung out ahead of the rest. Just like his disposition—smooth, synchronized with the world.

Robert's eleven-year-old had a crush on Jeff. Since I knew no other children, we'd visit the family at their suburban Simi Valley tract home (content as Jeff always was, I still *occasionally* entertained him). Little Madeline (yes, she was named after the character in the children's book) had decided she was going to marry him someday. This I heard through the other, younger daughter, in an apparently well-intentioned tattletale over the phone one evening after Jeff and I had returned from a barbecue at their home.

Ursula (no, I don't know who she was named after, sounds like some sci-fi thing though) calmly explained that Madeline had special powers and could reach inside Jeff's soul and command him to be hers. I remember chuckling a little; this was all the more ridiculous because Robert and his wife were on this thing where they didn't let their kids watch TV, to keep the world at bay I suppose. So somehow, these girls were able to fabricate these what? sex-slave fantasies? I remember it was such a big thing too, the TV ban. And the girls were put in some fundamentalist Baptist school, and everything else they read or saw was screened and censored. Their home video collection consisted entirely of Disney and fluff like the Smurfs. Please. Madeline was growing tits. But I didn't say anything; the parents had gone off the deep end before. The previous time it had been a nudist camp in Topanga, where they'd spent the summer with the girls. Needless to say, these two little brats were about as screwed up as anybody.

So I thanked Ursula for the important information and hung up, still chuckling. Jeff was reading some book about South America; I sure wasn't going to bore him with the story; he'd been fighting off little girls already as long as he could remember. And no, he didn't have a swollen ego about all of that. He never understood why people made a fuss about him, or anything for that matter. He just glides through life like he's on tracks nobody else can see, like they're underwater or something, and only he knows they're there. Everybody else has to fend for himself, and he gets this extra tool from God. Well, I'm glad he's the chosen one; I sure as hell haven't met anybody else who deserves. Anyway, I'm getting off on a tangent here again.

Jeff's stay that year was a long one—his parents having some major row, the one that became the divorce. So a few more weeks went by, and we decided on another visit to the family. Linda would be there too, maybe a few writers; we could all sit around and scrutinize each other's latest work, make it a working lunch. That's how Linda connived me into going. I'd pretty much already had it with these people. I was getting older. I'd been in LA long enough. Robert was really starting to piss me off. I didn't want to see his little girls again. I was enjoying just being with Jeff. But we went anyway.

Madeline swung open the door and yanked Jeff in, leaving me standing in the dust staring at little Ursula, who rolled her eyes as if to tell me her sister was a fruitcake. As if I didn't already know. Then the group around the dining table beckoned me in. Dozens of empty Starbucks cups littered the table. There was Robert; his wife (looking more haggard each time I'd see her); Linda, of course, in black leather pants and a turquoise halter (after turning forty she'd decided to join the millions of other LA women who dress younger than their age and look like complete morons. But at least she'd ditched the warmers by then); and three faux academic-looking men with the unshaven crust and pallid complexion often associated with *real* writers. Of course, these three—Mo, Curly, and whatever the other one's name was—hadn't washed their smelly clothes or showered recently either. Yikes.

One of them, Curly I think, was reading a stream-of-consciousness thing, which went on for about three freakin' hours. During hour two, I excused myself for the bathroom; and while standing and pissing, I happened to catch a peek of Madeline and Jeff outside, through the mini window above the toilet. They were sitting in some silly swinging bench, little distance between them. I finished pissing but stayed, fascinated by the body language of this rather *tart* female, who was obviously coming on to Jeff. He kept looking off to one side, then the other, as if hunting for some distraction; but there wasn't even a ball to pick up and toss. He was trapped. Suddenly Madeline leaned onto Jeff, catching him off guard in his desperate search for that ball and clasped his face between her hands. She pulled him almost violently toward her and pressed her lips to his, in what must have been a very painful what? kiss? Jeff squirmed slightly at first, as if trying to be polite; but, as the kiss continued, he made a more forceful effort to extract himself. As he pulled back, Madeline grabbed his crotch and groped the poor kid very aggressively, it must have hurt.

Jeff, smooth as ever, simply stood and walked toward the house. I ducked underneath the window, not wanting to embarrass him. The others wouldn't have seen anything; the dining room window faced the opposite side of the house. And who knows where the little bitch Ursula was. I suspected she was watching from some clandestine lair.

I quickly returned to the group and sat down as Jeff entered the house through a side door. Nobody looked up, Curly was involved in the protagonist's epiphany part of the story; smoke filled the air; these people thought they were beatniks or something. But I could see Jeff was a little ruffled, as ruffled as he ever got, which wasn't much. Not enough to say anything. He merely found a book and began to read. I felt bad and gave the group only ten minutes or so more; then we excused ourselves and mercifully left.

I didn't say anything on the way home. I figured Jeff would tell me if it was a big deal. But he didn't. What was there to say? Some little girl had put the make on him? So what else was new? Though I kind of wished he would have. If only to let him know I thought that whole scene to be downright creepy. But he probably already knew that. One thing about Jeff was you found yourself not wanting to bad-mouth people in his presence. He never did, being a saint and all. So things *had* to go unsaid. You could talk about how such and such wasn't right, that kind of thing. But you couldn't say such and such was an asshole. And since that's all I could think of to say, I just didn't say anything.

No longer than five minutes after we'd returned, Robert called, hysterical. You could hear his wife screaming in the background too, wailing almost, like someone had died, which I thought was what had happened. Then I could hear the girls join in; everybody was screaming and crying. I could hear them all clearly; they were all alive. What could be the problem? And why were they calling me? If the house was burning down, why didn't they call the fire department? Eventually, I could make out words.

"That fucking little brat tried to rape my daughter." Robert was screaming.

"What?" I asked. Even though I'd just witnessed the whole backyard seduction, it didn't occur to me he was talking about the same thing. Maybe because it wasn't the freakin' same thing?

"You heard me," he said. There were some especially loud wails in the background. For effect, I suppose. Loudest of all was Madeline now; I could make out her Academy Award–winning performance above the others.

"Calm down, and tell me what you are talking about," I said. I was beginning to grasp what was happening. My face must've turned red. I turned to Jeff; he was back on his book and hadn't looked up. But how could I keep this from him?

After a few moments in which Robert seemed to be composing himself, during which I listened as the house behind him relaxed, until I could hear only his apelike breathing, he finally spoke again.

"I never want that boy over here again. I should call the police, but because you're a friend I won't. But you better watch that animal. He's filthy; don't let that quiet act fool you."

I suppose I should have, if I could have, made some counterclaim, especially since I knew the truth. But I didn't. Looking back, I think most of it was Jeff, his influence on me, to not let those things which you cannot change control you, destroy you. I knew that nothing I could say would change Robert's mind. It was his daughter's word against Jeff's and mine. And, as I've said, I was already over those people. They exhausted me. This almost conveniently forced the issue. How fucked up is that? So, for the moment, I let it go. It was all so simple; I just said fine to Robert on the phone and hung up. Jeff looked at me and asked what was that about, and I just said it was some girl I knew with PMS (which I suppose *was* partly true); and he nodded politely and went back to his book.

But, about a year later, I did write a letter to Robert. We hadn't spoken since; and with Jeff being gone, I was (to my disadvantage) less influenced by his Zenlike approach to everything. It was a simple letter, not incendiary, at least I didn't think so. In about two paragraphs I described what I had seen (I left out the aggressiveness, even the crotch grab, concentrating more on the kiss and who seduced who) and suggested that his daughter was simply embarrassed or hurt. I didn't touch on the more dire concerns that she was vengeful, scheming, and even horny. I did suggest whatever happened was perfectly normal, along the line of kids experimenting, playing doctor, that sort of innocent thing. I was trying to be diplomatic, even though I knew Madeline was a bad seed.

Robert curtly wrote me back that the incident was still very fresh in the family's mind and that it was way too soon for any reconciliation (I hadn't wanted that!); and, in fact, Madeline couldn't possibly have had anything to do with "sexual or emotional experimentation" because she wouldn't know what it was, because they didn't have a TV! And he would never, as long as he lived, believe otherwise; and if I ever brought it up again, he would rethink filing charges and, at the very least, never speak to me again. Jesus.

—

Now, Linda wanted to call Robert over to look at the script.

"What the fuck for?" I continued.

"Please don't use that language in my home," Linda said. "You couldn't possibly still be angry about the Jeff thing?"

"No, I'm not," I said. Which was mostly true. I'd seen him a few times since then (the last time a couple of years prior—at the Venice party). No big deal; he was still an asshole.

"I just don't see the point," I said.

"Didn't you know?" Linda asked, as if about something that had been on TV every night and on the front page of the newspaper.

"Know what?"

"Robert . . ." And here there was a long pause, like she'd just said God's name, and we were supposed to revere it for a moment.

". . . is working for a reader at Sony," she finished. Then I was supposed to shit a brick or something, at least smother her with sloppy kisses; but all I could think of was, *Just my luck, the someone who knows someone who knows someone is the asshole.*

"Uh, great," I managed.

"You are still mad about that, aren't you," Linda said. She looked at me as if it was the most incredulous thing she'd ever heard.

"It's *not* that big a deal," I reemphasized.

Linda got up and towered over me as if to make a point. "You must get over this. You are carrying this negative energy far too long. This kind of stuff eats at you from the inside and eventually *devours* you. So get over it. This is business. We can use his input."

"Okay, Dr. Laura," I said.

"I'm serious," she glared.

"Obviously," I said.

Linda went for the phone.

—

Two days later, I was back at Linda's, this time for a powwow with her and Robert. She'd reached him on the phone immediately during my previous visit; and though I could only hear her side of the conversation, consisting mostly of one-syllabic grunts like oh, well, and sure, it was obvious he was as enthused about the rendezvous as I was. Although he must have perked up when Linda maintained the script was "very salable," (tossed out like bait, after she'd exhausted all the usual salvos about fine artistry, taut writing, three-dimensional characters). Linda's eyes lit up then, and she gave me the A-okay signal with her thumb and forefinger. Liked we'd scored some major Hollywood coup. Jesus. Seems Robert, in his golden years, had finally come around, like the rest of us, to see that all that really mattered was the money.

I arrived first and slouched through a remarkably similar visit with Linda before Robert arrived, right down to her paisley (I wondered if the building had a laundry room) and incense. Thankfully, Joni had been replaced by Judy Collins (little joke there). The tea, some herbal concoction with little brown thingies floating in it, was a *little* better, I had to admit; and I received it in an adult's cup this time—but still . . . my Linda quotient had already been used up for the year the other day; and I was beginning to rethink my strategy as we sat on the sofa waiting, Linda's sweaty feet (she wasn't wearing stockings this time) just itching to ram themselves under my thighs, when the knock came at the door.

Ta-da! There he was. I wanted to laugh, but I somehow suppressed it by pretending some tea had gone down my windpipe (which it then did, of course) and spitting it out over the spotless coffee table. While Linda, in a panic, ran to the kitchen for a rag (and likely Windex, ammonia, and spot remover, in case errant spit had reached the floor or sofa), I was left alone with what had to be history's most ill-advised result of bodybuilding. Really, if I could think of the words, I'd use them. Believe me, there aren't any. I stood face to face with someone who'd apparently modeled himself after one of those plastic He-Man dolls. Only, he'd forgotten about the legs; and, wearing shorts, he looked like Mr. Potato Head stuck on two straws, plus he was clearly now wearing a toupee. *And* he'd been in the tanning booth every day for about the past eight years. Which is not a good thing to do when you're fifty, as he must have been by then. *And* he'd taken to wearing gaudy gold jewelry like some porn producer. Great weighty strands of—what do you call them anyway? necklaces? chains?—were wrapped around his grizzled neck. *And* as if the caricature wasn't complete enough, he was wearing a silk shirt opened to reveal a grayish tuft of chest hairs on which the jewelry nested.

The choking act seemed to have worked, though I wondered if he noticed people were always spitting up around him (they had to have been—even in LA). I shook his hand, which felt like a dead fish, and we exchanged some ridiculous pleasantries. For some reason, he started on about Ursula and Madeline, what they were doing, how pretty they'd both become, just like their mother (he avoided an update on her—I knew they'd been divorced years earlier). Like I gave a shit. I knew exactly what kind of women they were—I saw them every day around town. I wondered what kind of game this guy was playing right off, but I quickly saw his eyes were vacant as a ghost's; he was just mindlessly repeating some spiel he told any schmuck he ran into these days. Too many steroids probably.

"That's nice," I said as I smiled and nodded, wondering what Linda was doing in the kitchen. I heard clanging, like pots and pans, then running water, then, sure enough, out from the nook she popped with a sudsy pot and sponge. She kneeled on the floor and began blotting out the already-absorbed tea.

"Darn," she said, near tears.

"You can't even see it," I said. Which was true, except for when she instantly found one of those floating thingies and proved me wrong. She approached it cautiously as though it was a maggot or something and lifted it into the bucket.

"I just cleaned in here," she mumbled superfluously. She seemed to finish with the tea spot and began to hunt for offensive dust particles. As long as she was there.

Robert and I just stood and watched, until I couldn't take it anymore. I made a couple of inexplicable comments about how he was "looking good" and "sure had been a long time." He nodded and fumbled through his shorts' pockets for whatever pills he took, popped a couple in his mouth; and soon we were on the sofa with the script on his lap, Linda on the floor doggie style between us.

"Let's see what you got here," Robert said, as he pulled a large red marker out of his shirt pocket. I glanced at him hesitantly as he began. What the fuck was I doing?

But, I have to admit, at the *very* beginning I was a *little* impressed at how proficiently he went through the script, economical but firm with those first few corrections, mechanical in style. He knew what he was doing. The pen slashed its way across a few pages, but through nothing that concerned me greatly. My baby was mostly intact after the first skimming. I relaxed, began to let my guard down, and ignored all my animal instincts, which had rightfully screamed warning earlier. There's a *huge* character flaw of mine, denying my consistent, almost psychic intuition. It doesn't matter how many times in great and dour circumstances I have ignored that feeling—the sense that something is wrong, like when a dog knows an earthquake's coming—I still brush it off.

By the time Robert had finished with the first reading, Linda had abandoned her search for dirt and was cozied up between us, saying things like "did you like that?" and "should we keep that?" Robert ignored her every time, as he flipped through the pages, as if she was a bothersome child.

Finally, he tossed the script on the table.

"Change the title," he said like the voice of the Almighty.

I thought I'd misunderstood. Did he mean change the CD?

"What?" I asked.

Linda looked at him, then me, then started to nod her head. First, she lifted it ever so slightly, then she picked up speed—like one of those bobbing springheads people put on their dashboards—until she was shaking like at a revival meeting. Apparently, she'd seen the light.

"Of course," she said. "It was right in front of us."

"What was?" I called her bluff.

"The title. It was all wrong," Linda said.

There was silence as we both looked to Robert for instructions. Here I must have been brainwashed a little, I know I looked like a cult member waiting for his Kool-Aid.

"Dr. Grim," Robert finally said.

Silence. A very long silence.

It was good; I'll give him that. I will give him the name, as I would give anybody his due. My head was spinning; there was so much weight placed on the replacement of a single letter, an adjacent letter at that. Of course, I fell for it, who wouldn't?

Linda clasped a hand over her mouth as if she'd just heard the meaning of life or opened a briefcase containing millions of dollars (which she had, as you shall see).

Robert explained it slowly then, as if I was too stupid to realize what it all meant. I mean, I only *wrote* the fucking thing.

"I can see where you're going with this Dr. Grin thing," he said. "And that's good too, really good in fact. I mean, the guy smiles all the time, and he thinks he's doing good for the planet and all that. Very *Pleasantville* meets *Invasion of the Body Snatchers*. But *Dr. Grim* is even better, it's . . . *fantastic*, if you don't mind me saying so. Think of it."

Robert took his hands and pantomimed a box, as if it would be easier for me to grasp on TV. His chains were all dangling furiously now, in concert with the bonanza of the moment. Beads of sweat covered his forehead. I wondered if he had a heart condition and if the excitement might kill him.

"Are you okay?" I asked. He was becoming drenched, the sweat dripping down his neck.

"Oh, I'm fine. Don't worry about it. It's just the pills."

No worries there. Jesus. Except for how fine that line was between me just getting the hell out (I was *this*close then. Damn!) and continuing on. (See above for my thoughts on drug-addled Hollywood types.)

Needless to say, we continued. Linda quickly went for a tissue as Robert took a minute or so to get it together. He dabbed his face and neck delicately with the Kleenex and arranged himself more comfortably on the sofa, even doing a little crotch adjusting, as if those pills had some effect on his penis too. Before long, we'd returned to the screenplay, now *Dr. Grim*.

Linda sat quietly by for most of the rest of the evening, letting Robert steal the show. She tossed in a few thoughts; but they seemed forced, as if she was obligated because I'd originally called her or whatever. Who knew what these two were up to? Hindsight again. I guess I thought about it once, real casually, that they must've had some preliminary talk, a plan of attack. But, remember, I already said I didn't follow my instincts too well. And I didn't really intuit malice, just premeditation of some sort. Looking back, I can see they both thought I was a stupid fuck. Linda played the baby-doll act she'd mastered, so I'd be ambushed easier. It was pretty smooth; and for a while, this first night with Robert, I felt like we were just our dumbass threesome again. I even had some weepy story ideas while sitting there, about how three old friends get together after years of estrangement and write a successful script together and become friends and live happily ever after. Really demented, pathetic stuff like that.

Robert suggested a few more changes that night, which I agreed to. Just some composition stuff; we changed a few words. There was very little done. Okay, we *did* change the scene where Dr. Grim tells the human nurse (he's in love with) who he is. That whole storyline was excessive, I agreed. It confused the issue, became another whole plot, like a love story. I agreed it was better that Dr. Grim carry his lonely secret, so we didn't even have him tell her he loved her. The unrequited carrying-a-torch thing added more depth to his character, a smoldering even; and the waters weren't muddied with a story about an alien and an earthling. But that was really the only other significant change of the night.

When we finished at 4:00 AM the script still remained mostly intact. I let Robert take it, of course; that was the whole point. We left together. It was a sight watching him put on his shoes in the hallway. After a couple attempts, he had to sit down to do it—right there in the hall. Linda had already shut the door behind us like she was sick of us, or we were a couple stray mutts or something. We walked to our cars side by side as if we were chums again; it was *very* deranged.

Then, Robert got into a Volkswagen beetle (an original from about 1969), for cryin' out loud. I would have figured him for a grossly oversized SUV, but I supposed that was beyond his budget. (He still lived in Sunland—we'd touched on that for a second.) There was another laughable moment when he squeezed into the bug like one squeezes into a wet suit, but I gave it a rest. I was tired, and he might have even looked such a case I pitied him. Okay, that's pushing it, maybe not pity exactly, more like it was too easy. Give me something harder to work with.

—

I arrived home that night to find my apartment had been burglarized. The door was kicked in, one large hole clear through. Anybody who wanted to could've kneeled and peered inside, where my scattered writer's belongings laid strewn indigenously about. Piles of books, trade newspapers, pizza boxes, soda cans, overflowing ashtrays, empty beer bottles. The whole nine yards. I lived like that, I admit it. It comes with the territory—both territories really, an artist's life and broke in Hollywood.

But they wouldn't have seen my computer, because it was gone. And they wouldn't have seen my thumb drives or CDs because they were gone too. I supposed the thief took those—in case struggling screenwriters' original drafts had some value on the Hollywood Boulevard black market. (As it ultimately turned out, a cynical but not-altogether far-fetched notion.)

I looked up and down the hallway; almost a parody of poverty. Lone light bulb dangling from a frayed cord, cracked and crumbling plaster from earthquakes, water damage, domestic disputes; tattered carpet runner (really just old padding, the top rug long ago worn to shreds), and the sickening, permanent odor from decades of cooking all mixed up into one giant goulash. Jesus.

What did I think I was going to do? Knock on a neighbor's door and ask in Aberjanistani if they'd seen anything? Would they even answer? Would they answer with an AK-47? I'd seen the man across the hall; he looked like he'd been fighting the Russians over in Chechnya. One eye covered in an outsized patch, the distinct mark of a bullet through his left cheek. It had perversely fascinated me at the time. I briefly pondered using his world-weary story in a script. Until I imagined the interview: He and I cuddled up in some lounge, sipping cognac, as he relayed to me the horrible suffering his family had experienced. One child blown to bits by a land mine in front of him, his wife had lost a leg, the other child kidnapped by guerrillas and forced to work for the rebels, far up in the frozen hills, cleaning latrines and stealing cows. I'd smile and nod like some TV news cretin, feigning like I gave a shit, when all I really cared about were high ratings and good hair days.

I decided not to bother the neighbors. I cried instead, which might have brought them out anyway if tremendous heaving convulsions by a grown man had been anything out of the ordinary. But they'd heard all that before from any number of residents withdrawing from any number of things. Maybe they were just surprised the guy in 201 had taken so long to either start on or run out of the smack.

I sobbed and retched for a good five minutes out there in that disgusting hallway until I saw that somebody had recently taken a piss right against the wall. Then I sadly stepped into my *violated* apartment. I'd been mugged before; I knew that feeling, but, really, how the fuck could I feel any more infiltrated in that dump? We were all so right on top of each other I knew when somebody downstairs took a piss.

Once inside, I cursed and blamed everybody else for the woeful predicament. First off, my parents, of course, for not paying for college so I'd have a good *real* job. Then, the president for the economic downturn, then the drug war for its focus on imprisonment not rehabilitation, then immigrants, Hollywood, age, art, and on and on until I stopped dead in my tracks.

Suddenly, I realized I did not have a copy of *Dr. Grim*. I'd only made one paper copy, figuring I'd make multiples when it had been edited. The master had been on my hard drive. I used an older version of Microsoft WORD so my work wasn't in the cloud yet. The only proof of the script's existence was in Robert's clammy hands. Shit.

This was a very rare lapse for me. Years earlier, a friend had a similar crisis when his home had burned to the ground, literally. I don't know what the fuck the place was made of—cardboard or something—but there was *nothing* left. He'd been a successful photographer and a fledgling novelist, and he lost *everything* he'd ever worked on. Like me, he'd had a library of unpublished stuff he kept at home in filing cabinets. All gone. (Yes, the fire had been so intense it melted the metal cabinets.) The guy was devastated; it had the effect on his marriage that losing a child does. They divorced soon after. (It had been a good marriage.) He took to drinking heavily, finally left town, and moved to Reno with his mother, where he now works on layout for the *Reno Gazette*. Very sad. I visited him once; he looked ten years older than he is. He said he couldn't write anymore, and he gambles and chain-smokes.

Anyway, since then, in addition to the file cabinet in my closet, which held a hard copy of everything I'd ever written, I'd put discs and flash drives in safe deposit boxes, registered and deposited copies with the Writers Guild, and copyrighted everything. *But* I just hadn't gotten around to all that with *Dr. Grim* yet. Jesus, I had just finished the first draft days prior. (No excuse, I know).

I vainly tore through my garbage, looking for an earlier copy I had made that had printed smeared, which I knew I'd thrown out in the bin, but still . . . Or maybe the burglar had decided against the worthless drives and tossed 'em?

Yeah right. (Though he had deposited a Big Mac wrapper, apparently having decided to eat on the job).

Eventually, after more tears, I decided to come fully around, as Jeff would have, and be thankful that I'd made the one copy and look at everything through some sickeningly optimistic lens (sorry Jeff). So I began to make myself feel a little better—drank some milk, smoked a cigarette. The retching had helped too. And I discovered just before passing out at dawn, the literate thief had taken a couple of bound earlier works of mine left on my desk, which I'd printed just for the hell of it one day when I'd had too much coffee. So it was a good thing Robert had the only copy, right? Then why was I so disturbed?

—

I fell into a profound sleep then, which no amount of Hollywood din outside my window could disturb, until midafternoon, when I bolted from bed like a switch had been thrown. I had had another script idea during that sleep, another wicked dream, my subconscious ready to fight before I even knew there was a fight to be had.

This was to be another masterpiece. I could feel it; there was no doubt in my mind. There was a machination in my movements that day, a destiny so irreversible I was placed on its course like a fryer on an assembly line belt. There was no getting off. I didn't have a choice. I didn't have the power. I was being maneuvered like a marionette. It was dropped into my sleep like a shroud over a corpse. A perfect story, even more perfect than **Dr. Grim**, but one which needed the doctor to give birth. A story that only the doctor could yank out of the womb, abruptly, coldly, into a world ambiguous about its arrival, yet soon to acknowledge its importance, even its *majesty*.

I quickly dressed, a man obsessed, and headed to a nearby print shop with a rental computer. I needed to write. And I did, all afternoon, evening, and into the next morning. I didn't eat or drink; I just pounded feverishly away at ten bucks an hour. Thousands of words I wrote, and I had more; but I ran out of money. Then something walked me home; some unseen companion had me by the arm, put the door key in my fingers, twisted the lock, led me to the fridge, placed bologna on some bread, and crammed it in my mouth. Something moved my teeth, causing me to chew. Something reached for a glass, poured milk with my hands, and brought the glass to my mouth. Something allowed the milk to coat my stomach. Something lifted my sweater over my head and brought my jeans to my ankles.

Something removed my shoes, pulled the jeans off. Something pushed me back on the bed and reached for my eyelids and brought them down over my blood red eyes. Something made me sleep.

I slept for twenty-four hours, losing an entire day before waking at dawn to the sounds of birds singing, for God's sake. In the ghetto? The only birds usually alive in that part of Hollywood were crows. Ravens, specifically. Satan's henchmen guarding their kingdom.

But these were simple (obviously lost and soon to be gorged) starlings or sparrows or something. Innocent little things perched outside my window. As if it were perfectly normal for them to be just chatting away another day in hell.

Well, what did that mean? What great poignant moment was I meant to have? I suppose just seeing dawn from the right side up was something. Dawn of a new day; maybe it was that simple. Then I remembered the new screenplay and the missing one and thought I'd better get my shit together. I opened the window; and the birds flew off back to Shangri-La or wherever they live; and a couple of crows cawed loudly nearby. And I knew the world was right again. Just a little glitch, that was all.

—

I had to call Linda about the problem—I didn't have Robert's number yet; why hadn't I asked for that?—but it was barely 6:00 AM. I could be civil, I supposed, at least in real life. They were certainly facing foreboding circumstances in their fictitious lives, for the first draft of the new story had characters patterned after both of them already on painful journeys to the abyss. But I didn't wait long. With all that sleep in me, I was raring to go, a new man. I showered, dressed, even shaved. I taped some cardboard over the hole in the door. (Yes, I had let it be those two days. I didn't give a damn; I was depressed.) Add a pot of coffee and I barely made it to seven before dialing Linda.

"Hi, may your spirit soar and the cosmos embrace, and may your day be peaceful and bliss. Please leave a message after the beep," the voicemail said. Linda's voice dropped precipitously after *bliss*, and she deadpanned the leave-a-message part as though she recorded the two halves on different days or someone had rushed her out of the apartment. Anyway, it was a new recording, and it was perfect. I couldn't make something like that up. I'd use it in my new story, in the scene where the protagonist calls his so-called friend about his screenplay, and she's gone to Vegas with the other so-called friend who just sold the script claiming it as his own. It would be the new message ex-friend number 1 had on her voicemail.

Okay, so she was probably sleeping. Whatever. I asked her to call Robert first thing that morning to tell him I had my computer stolen; he had the only copy of *Dr. Grim*, and I needed it back. Now, here you might think I was out of my mind, right? But what precedent did I have? What does anyone do in a situation like that? I don't care how long you live in Hollywood, or how long you live *anywhere*; it takes a royal assfuck to become unwaveringly convinced that *everybody* is out to screw you, even your friends. So, for the moment, give me the benefit of the doubt. I was just naive. Jesus.

Even if I was already busy writing a new script remarkably like the real shenanigans? Yes, that was different. A whole other world goes on in my creative life. How was I to know such an overlap was possible, even with my strange sleeping disorder? Anyway, I jotted the phone message scene down on my tablet, swigged some milk (by then I was starting to have stomach problems, in case you're wondering about all the milk I was drinking—I'd had an ulcer once before, I was trying to be careful) and headed out the door.

I thought about the print shop again, but figured I might as well overdraw my bank account and get a used computer somewhere. I'd cover it with my next unemployment check. (I'd temped six months for a tattoo parlor; they'd laid me off.) I was due for a few more—sure to get me through to the end of this new idea, which I was calling *Final Draft*. And if *Dr. Grim* wasn't my ticket out, I was convinced *Final Draft* would be. Then, flush with cash, my dream was to buy a house on Lake Tahoe, the east side, facing the mountains and the sunset. Or even Pasadena, as long as it was far away from LaBrea Avenue. Okay, so I was going off on a tangent that morning. A guy can dream, can't he?

On Hollywood Boulevard, the pawnshops were just opening, their prisonlike gates loudly hoisted up by dark-skinned Mideasterners seemingly oblivious to the sleeping homeless camped out in all manner of fashion faux pas. It occurred to me, as I entered one urine-soaked breezeway, that I may actually find my computer, serial number expertly replaced, hard drive erased of my brilliance. I hoped not, somehow convinced I would burst into tears again at the sight of my defiled loved one.

I needn't have worried. There were literally hundreds of used models in this place; I couldn't have picked mine out if I tried. I knew there was a police procedure these places followed; I'd actually temped in a pawnshop for a while. There was a whole ID thing, lots of forms, detectives that came around regularly to check on stolen property, matching docket numbers, the whole bit. But none of that could convince me. I knew most of these computers were *not* legitimately pawned; I don't care how many starving writers Hollywood has. There are many more junkies, runaways, homeless, prostitutes looking to ditch their pimps, gangbangers, and—well, you get the picture.

The grizzled, toothless proprietor eyed me suspiciously, as I supposed he did everybody. I meandered to one sagging shelf of ancient Macs, then moved on. I had always used a PC. Nearby was a row of laptops, which I'd assumed were beyond my budget. I humored myself by checking a fading price tag, which read $295.00. I assumed it was either mismarked or not working, so I asked.

"Is this right?"

"What's the problem over there?" the man said. Like I was creating a scene. He walked quickly toward me, his mouth puckered with distaste, his eyes glaring.

I wasn't in the mood for this shit.

"I just asked if the price was correct on this," I said.

"What's wrong with it? Too high for you? Go down the street then, see if you can do better. They got shit there; that's what they got. Me, I stand by what I sell here." He reached the laptop as he said this and read the price.

"That's a good price. Everybody always wants a deal. Everybody try to Jew me down."

Well, this pissed me off.

"Look, you don't need to be a bigot about this. I never said anything was wrong with the price. I'm just asking a question."

We stared each other down for a moment. I was thinking about buying it, but I have this weird thing where the *vibe* has to be right. (Look, if I could think of some other word I would, but I have to use it because nothing else works.) It's important to me that some episode not taint the art I'm going to create on the thing. I know, I know it's stupid; it's almost as stupid as some of Linda's new age shit. It really puts me in the league doesn't it? But I can't help it; I do have some of the *artiste* thing in me. I'm not trying to cover this shit up. I'm trying to be about as factual as I can with this story. I can be neurotic sometimes. There, I said it. Let's move on.

"I just haven't bought a computer in a while and thought good laptops were pricier," I said, in a spirit of cease-fire.

"What? You wanna pay more, fine with me," this guy said. Jesus.

"Does it work?" I asked.

"Course it works. You think I sell the shit? That's what these things go for now. Used anyway. Market is glutted."

"All right, all right. I'll take it." I surrendered. What the fuck did I know except I wanted to get the hell out of there.

"Give me a minute though." I glared at him. I'd be writing my ticket out of this sewer on it; I wanted to figure out how it worked. There was a little manual attached to it by a paperclip. I started to read it as he walked to his desk.

"Three hundred twenty-three twenty-eight," he called back. "With tax."

I fondled the gray box a few seconds before opening it and flipping on the power. A magical wonderland appeared before me in swirling musical colors. Microsoft Windows, with Word already installed. I could see the icon beckoning me like the star of freakin' David. Okay, so I was getting carried away, but I was *extremely* excited; I'd always wanted a laptop. It was the freedom thing. I'd envied those hipsters (is that still the correct term, or have I been in my cave too long?) sitting in coffee houses clicking away at their stories, while I was balled and chained to my hole.

I went all through the booklet, discovering a universe I'd been denied. Though it was an old model, in technology years that only meant four or five years; everything could be done with this thing. It ran on a battery, or with the AC adapter, even on a 12-volt in my car. Now there's something—me sitting in my car looking up at Half Dome or anywhere out of the freakin' city, typing away. It could hook up to my printer (oddly not taken by the thief), attach to a larger screen; it even had a modem. If I wanted to get on the Internet, I could become one of those blogger types if I felt like it, mindlessly conversing with complete strangers about every idiotic thing there was. Reading their opinions as if I gave a shit.

Model HP XP. More beautiful letters were never written (except of course those that were about to be on said HP). I paid the creep and tucked the thing under my arm, where it fit snugly. This was going to be great! I walked quickly off the boulevard and headed home, where I would be for about three seconds, just long enough to try Linda again and grab my car keys.

—

But Linda still didn't answer. So I left her another message, this time emphasizing the urgency, and sat down on my squeaky bed. I searched every obscure corridor of my overburdened brain to recall what exact office Robert worked at, to no avail. Had he even told me? Then I tried to remember his home landline phone, which I'd purposely deleted from my brain years earlier. No good. Then I tried calling Sony. Just *Sony*. Well, that was a joke.

"Sony Music," said a pleasant voice.

"Hi, do you have a general script development department?" I asked pathetically.

"Who are you trying to reach, sir?"

"Well, his name is Robert Simmons; he works for a reader. I don't know which office."

"This is Sony Music, in Santa Monica."

"No, sorry," I said. "I need Sony Studios, or wherever they do TV and film." God, I was an idiot, wasn't I? You're probably figuring out that even though I'd spent twenty years in the cesspool, I had *never* called a studio. No need to, okay? After all, my scripts were molding in a closet; it's not as if they were on anybody's desk. Not until now anyway.

"I'll have to know where to transfer you, sir."

"No, listen, can you just give me the number to the studio?"

"That's 310-244-4000."

"Thanks," I said. Then I dialed the new number.

"Sony Studios," someone said.

For a moment, I got revved up, real impressed; my heart might have skipped a beat even. It was a *very* minute version of how I'd felt many years earlier whenever I came in contact with anybody or anything that had to do with *the business*. I was the worst of the worst of the gushing, fawning wannabes then. Now my greatest wish was to leave town, but for a second, just a second, I was reminded of how I'd felt once.

"Do you have a general office for readers?" I asked.

"Well, that might be story development, but I'll have to have a name. Can you hold, please?"

I held for seven minutes, listening to the extended dance remix of Barry Manilow's "Looks Like We Made It." There was drool on the receiver when the person finally returned.

"Sorry," she said. In fairness, I have to say—since this is a true story—that the people at Sony *seemed* nice; they were just doing their jobs. Nobody was snotty. None of these people on the phone acted like a princess, none of that. It's just that they couldn't help me. Rules were rules.

"It's okay," I said. "I was holding for story development."

"Thank you, I'll transfer you now."

"Story," someone said. There was barely a ring; I thought I was finally getting somewhere.

"Hi," I said meekly. "I am looking for someone, and I don't know where he works, except that I know he works for a reader at Sony."

"Well, they're called story analysts; but we can't transfer to them."

"Can I get a message to somebody."

"No, sir, I don't have the authority to do that."

"Well, he's not even one of your people; he just *works* for one of your people."

I guess I was starting to sound desperate. I can imagine what kinds of calls these people must get all day, every day.

"No, sir. There is no way I can help you."

"Well, if I just gave you a name would you say yes or no that you've heard of him?"

"No, sir, I really can't say anything. There are strict rules here."

"Could you just nod yes or no then?" I said, before hanging up.

I sat and stared into space for a few minutes. Until something very ominous happened.

I let it go.

Not for any new age reasons like, "what's meant to be is meant to be," or (another of my least favorites) "whatever doesn't kill you makes you stronger." (What bullshit artist made that one up? Somebody trying to console some poor guy who'd lost his entire family to marauding warriors or in a fire or something?) No, the reason was possibly even more paranormal. It was as if I had to let things happen to get the best story, so maybe there *was* a little bit of *whatever's meant to be* in there, but anyway.

I decided not to pursue Robert aggressively. We would meet again soon enough; I could feel it. So that meant no googling, facebooking, obsessively texting Linda, anything!

After that decision (and hopefully this isn't too weird), I can best describe the feeling I had as missing someone close to you. Only, of course, this was a *thing*, the script, but more than that . . . The characters had been such a large part of—okay—my *entire* life for so many months. Every single day, every waking and sleeping hour I spent with Dr. Grin (I still think of him that way) and Carol his compassionate nurse, and the warmhearted but doomed patients. I did miss them, is that crazy? When the script was around, I could fiddle with them a little every day, even after I was finished with the main body. I could make them say a different word here and there, make Carol stand closer to the doctor if I wanted, or give someone a haircut, make someone eat ice cream or dress a little better. Whatever. I was still with them every day; things were not yet firmly established. Imagine reading a book you love, and you never get to the end. It keeps coming; there is never that inevitable sadness when you finish and realize you won't be with those people, who you are now close to, anymore.

I finally had that sadness.

—

But there was no time to dwell. *Final Draft* beckoned. I needed to get a grip. And I could now join the legions of pretentious Hollywood types publicly writing their latest in Starbucks' all across town. I looked forward to it, If you can't beat 'em (which I certainly hadn't been able to) then you might as well . . . you get the picture.

So I parked myself at a little bistro table in a too-precious Internet cafe filled with all things country clutter—distressed, whitewashed hutches; raggedy Ann and Andy dolls; little wheelbarrows with rusted wheels in which quilted-type things were draped to look as if they'd been thrown in when you knew someone had spent hours trying to get that just-tossed look. All very unHollywood. Maybe it was supposed to be campy, though I didn't see how that worked. The staff was more typical Hollywood—piercings, ghoulish makeup, tattoos, blood, all the usual—so I wondered what mindfuck the owner was playing. But they had outlets for laptops, and it was right on Highland, where I could watch the people circus go by; so I spent the afternoon feeling *very* hip. And writing prodigiously.

That day, I whizzed through act 1. Back at the print shop, I had established the writer, Patrick, as the protagonist and the characters, Randy and Lisa, as the antagonists. Patrick had written a brilliant script, and Randy and Lisa were out to steal it. Patrick had to do something about that, didn't he? That was the simple premise, the mission of the protagonist that is supposed to become apparent in the first thirty pages of a well-written screenplay. I was using basic formula with this script, sticking directly with what I'd learned in screenwriting courses. (I'd veered from the predictability of that lately—*Dr. Grim* was stylistically full of industry no-nos—since my formulaic attempts had only gathered dust in the closet.)

I neatly arranged all the questions a director or producer would ask and then provided the answers with great broad strokes as if I were painting, not writing. My fingers even swept across the little keyboard as if they were brushes, my movements left to right rather than vertical. Everything came back to me as if I was still sitting in ancient Ms. Dark's Intro to Hollywood class, twenty years earlier. Surrounded by doe-eyed imbeciles (of which I was most definitely one), the teacher (they always had someone teach who'd written one B-movie script thirty-seven years ago) taught us that, in addition to introducing the protagonist and antagonist in act 1, a good writer should (in accordance with a textbook I've long since forgotten the name of) fulfill these basics:

A. Setting up the mood, tone, and setting. Well, that was easy. The mood and tone were smoldering vengeance in a dank Hollywood locale.

B. Why is the story important to us, the audience? What are the central questions and conflicts that will be explored? Easy too. It's textbook psychology that we all like to see the bad guy get his just reward. This will be a story about karma, about getting what one deserves, about what goes around comes around, all that crap.

C. Introduce the subplot. Here it wasn't a cut-and-dry matter. My story was *so* focused on Patrick getting revenge. If I had to have a B story, it would be that poor Patrick really wanted to get out of Hollywood, so, hopefully, the audience will root for him to do that and get his dream house in Colorado, or wherever. I hadn't gotten that far yet.

D. Introduce a *major* event that turns the protagonist's life around, challenges everything he wants in life, and launches him into act 2. That was the easiest of all. Somebody steals his freakin' script, the one he'd been working on for months, the one that might've finally propelled him out of his shithole life. That'll get the guy charged up for the next act, wouldn't you think?

Another day had gone by. I slipped in a voicemail-Vegas scene, and the first act was finished. And I'd taken better care of myself that day. Being in a cafe, I ate. It was a peculiar (they called it quaint) sandwich on focaccia bread. (They didn't have plain ol' bread.) There were slippery things on it like eels (they said they were exotic mushrooms) and radicchio (they didn't have any normal lettuce); but like I said, at least I ate. It was all very chichi. People came in and out and ordered these silly sandwiches, pronouncing them impeccably, the vowels rolling off their tongues like they were eating them already. *Penne, bene, bella, bellisimo* blah, blah. But I felt all right that day, even well. I hadn't felt really good in a long time and so that felt good, just being aware of that. I even forgot about the misadventures of the doctor for a while, if such a thing can be said. Is there a word for double irony?

—

Reality blindsided me when I walked into my dump, and my mood soured. How many days had it been? three? four? I called Linda again and heard the same fucking message. The cosmos would certainly not want to embrace me, and my spirits were not soaring. Plus, there's something about the stench of fresh urine on the front stoop and the sounds of a woman screaming.

I was pissed again. I would just have to send Linda a text. I'm not a frequent texter anyway as I still own an ancient flip-phone with the little keys, and frankly I shouldn't have had to be put in this position anyway. Perhaps I needed to send a harsh text then? I agonized over that for a while before deciding not yet. But I would change the message on my voicemail to reflect a more aggressive me. I made a few sample recordings, making sure they sounded aloof and disinterested. Unfortunately, my favorite, "What do you want? Beep," sounded too harsh for the literary agents I was sure would be calling soon. So I opted for "Leave a message. Beep." It said so much by saying so little.

I stayed home that night, waiting for Linda's call, which never came. Just before drifting off, I decided I'd try and see her directly tomorrow. And if she wasn't home, I'd drive out to Sunland; I could find that dive too, if I tried. Stick a note on his scummy door, something like, "Where's my script, dickbreath?"

This was also the night I first accepted Linda—maybe even both of them—were avoiding me. I stayed home for about fourteen hours straight, mostly watching my snowy old TV. Jerry Springer, Dr. Phil and some other really deranged stuff. And she never called.

—

By morning, I was livid. I awoke to no new messages or even a text, which meant that I hadn't missed a call deep within my sleep. It was time to step up the attack.

In Ms. Dark's course, the outline for act 2 was never to be deviated from. "The Protagonist encounters obstacles to his mission" was written in large script letters clear across her blackboard the entire semester. She convinced us that to deter from this *essential* rule would cause the audience to wander. And, she insisted, we must keep our audience in the throes of our story, on a roller coaster of highs and lows, expectations and surprises, escalating complications and increasingly serious confrontations in which, along the way, the stakes grow progressively higher and higher.

"This is to be the bulk of your story," Ms. Dark would emphasize. "This is where you have locked in your audience. They are at your mercy, on the edge of their seats, awaiting the outcome of this, your finest fucking writing hour." Or something like that. She probably didn't say the "fucking" part. But Ms. Dark was very melodramatic. I think the one script she'd sold was some tearjerker, costume-drama thing with Judy Holliday or Jane Wyman; I always get those two mixed up—whoever was in that 50s black-and-white version of *The Glass Menagerie*. Yes, Ms. Dark was *that* old.

Anyway, I was in the bulk of my story now.

I called Linda's number again, not expecting an answer. Of which there wasn't. So I methodically prepared for my day. Milk—we've been through that—a shower; I shaved again, believe it or not. And that morning, I did some weird little primate grooming, like squeezing hard-to-see blackheads, clipping my eyebrows and nose hairs, flossing, and stuff like that. Microgrooming that I rarely did. Some primal need for me to be fastidious? Maybe. Whatever it was, I was spic-and-span as I got into my less-than-so beater. So then I treated myself to a car wash at an overpriced Sunset Boulevard place where they park the Rolls and Mercedes out front when they're finished so people can ogle them and get their materialistic panties all wet as they drive by.

After I got all cleaned up I drove to Studio City.

Linda wasn't there, so I went back to the car for a pen and paper; and as I was writing, her neighbor came out, saw me, and said something about Linda having gone off to Laughlin for a few days.

"Are you sure it wasn't Vegas?" I asked.

"No," the smarmy snoop said. "It was Laughlin. I know because that feller who picked her up had a boat; they were goin' to the river."

"What did he look like?" I asked.

This guy glared at me like he'd said enough, like maybe I was her boyfriend whom she was now cheating on; and I'd just asked what scumbag she was poking.

"I don't know. I don't know her business," he said, inching away.

Oh, so now his nosy ass had ethics.

"Was he bald?" I asked, as he slipped through my fingers like the slime he was.

"I gotta go," he said, and he was down the hall and out the door. I pulled out the pad from my pocket and flipped back to the Vegas scene where I crossed it out. I made a note to change the location to The Edgewater Hotel, Laughlin, Nevada.

Needless to say, the note I left on Linda's door had an added flair after the chat with Snoopy. "Please call me, hope all is well." became "Linda. I was here. Call me NOW! Urgent."

Now, I didn't really know if she was with Robert. But she now had a friend with a boat; and nobody I knew knew anybody with a boat, so I was getting some pretty good act 2 obstacles going here. But the real flags still hadn't gone up. How could they have? This script had been out of my hands less than a week. What were the two of them going to do? Find a buyer and get a check within that time? hardly, right? but maybe? Something was up.

Because of its size in relation to the other acts, Ms. Dark believed act 2 should be broken into three parts. Part 1 was where the protagonist reacts to the challenge he's encountered. His major decision leads him into action; and as he faces this initial action, we see development. Sometimes, something happens that impedes the subplot, and we're given an inkling of what's to come.

Jesus, this script is practically writing itself. I reacted to this first challenge— the obvious disposal of me/Patrick as a player in the development of **Dr. Grim**— by writing the furious note. Don't think I was jumping the gun here; maybe for once I was acknowledging my intuition. The major decision was to somehow find these two. It was over. I couldn't trust them, right? The development is that I, I mean Patrick, finally wises up and sees just what is happening. As for the subplot being impeded and the inkling of what's to come, well, obviously, Patrick will not get out of his rat-infested slum if his one-way ticket has been taken. And you're on your own as to the hints of what's to come.

—

I left Linda's a bit dazed. Things were obviously getting convoluted; and I wondered if I wasn't too involved with the new script. Should I settle things first, maybe even head to the river, if only to pacify my paranoid demons? Or should I continue on my new wonderwork, with an uncharacteristic zeal to work, as long as I had it in me?

Let me clarify that: While I have always enjoyed, in a masochistic sense, expunging a story, the literal weight of the *idea* released (therefore it *exists*—something concrete, not just abstract), I have *never* enjoyed the act of writing, the endless hours peering at the screen hoping, waiting, for the words to come out right. The eyes like cherry tomatoes, the back like Quasimodo's, the skin like a cadaver's. All of that I hate. And the time especially. Writing a book, even a screenplay, takes a long time. Until I am very deep into the story, when I am *living* the story, I remain restless, even anxious, to go out and get a *real* life. It's too late now, of course. I have spent so many years hunched over the keyboard; it is my life. And the length of the piece is another sore spot. Most literary forms are designed to be of an approximate, even specific length. A good novel consists of at least 80,000 or 90,000 words, usually more. A novella is about half that, sometimes less. A screenplay is about 120 pages. A short story should be wrapped up in 10,000 or 15,000 words, preferably much shorter. There are format rules. (And don't get me started on poems and stanzas and lyrics and articles and all the other forms of writing I've done). It all makes me go batty with the word count tool. I'm never convinced about what I'm starting on, at least when it comes to fiction. Scripts are usually different. They begin as scripts, but even then I've switched midway to change it to a novel or whatever so oftentimes I'll hope to be starting work on a short story, figuring I'll wrap it up in a day or so. And six months later, I'm still laboring over some behemoth novel. Jesus.

So was it *Final Draft* itself or something deeper—the mutant birth thing I mentioned earlier—or something as simple as the new laptop that was inspiring me with this *desire* to work? or all of the above? Whatever it was, it was the balloon I plucked out of the sky that day; and I have never looked back.

Final Draft became my life.

Part Two

It was almost three weeks before I received a call from Linda. Even then, it was only a message on my voicemail. I knew she preferred it that way; I'd answered the phone two or three times during that period from unfamiliar numbers when the caller had hung up at my voice. It was Linda; I could feel her icy breath through the line. But I didn't scream out anything like "Linda! Linda! I know it's you." I was being cool about the matter, methodically preparing for the final act, which was *not* coming. To be completely honest, the script by then was coming along slowly, a trickle of words at the rate of only a hundred or so a day. But I was a patient man. What else did I have to do? Besides, to do it right took much preparatory work. I had to learn to think like the characters, which involved days and weeks of research, scheming, even masterminding. The screenplay had to be perfect if I was ever to escape Hollywood.

I knew that Linda had moved out of her studio; I'd driven by a few times, looking for plot ideas, wanting to stay *true* to the source. One day, as I sat parked across the street from her building the entire afternoon, munching stale AM/PM popcorn and guzzling orange sodas, intermittently tapping on my now-beloved laptop, I watched, fascinated, as a small moving van pulled up and within two hours had fully loaded Linda's meager belongings. I got a good laugh out of that and began to type furiously, glad to get some comic relief in the otherwise somber story.

Linda ran alongside the beleaguered moving men (really two boys working for college tuition or something) with every load. She wedged herself between walls and furniture, picking lint and dust off *as* they carried pieces, occasionally clasping her hands to her head, even covering her eyes, during a particularly painful moment. Like when the sofa was actually set into the freakin' truck. Big crises like that.

I could see the poor kids rolling their eyes clear from where I sat, easily fifty yards away. When they were finally finished, after Linda had inspected the ropes, was convinced the plastic sufficiently covered everything, had checked for cobwebs in the upper reaches of the truck box (*apparently*, what else was she doing poking her equine nose up into the far reaches? hunting for a hidden camera?), even patted down the boys for dust, they were finally off.

The funniest scene (I wrote an entire page here) was when Linda handed them a slip of paper, probably the new address, and ran back into the apartment for something. Though you could *tell* she wanted to follow or even lead them in her car, they tried to hightail it out of there by quickly jumping into the cab. I watched as one kid fumbled hilariously with the keys, as his friend yelled, "Shit! Go! Hurry!" Finally the kid got the key in the ignition, the diesel engine started with a shake and a rumble, black smoke spewed out of the rear exhaust; and he jerked the truck into the street almost broadsiding an ancient man in the smallest car available to American buyers. What was that? A golf cart? Do they even allow those on busy streets? The old guy, completely unfazed, merely tooted his little horn and swerved to avoid the truck. Which now roared off.

Just then, Linda came running onto the sidewalk yelling for the kids to wait, which they didn't. She looked up then down the street, as if she was expecting somebody, then back at the truck, now fast disappearing toward Ventura Boulevard. Then she ran to a gleaming new Lexus parked two spots back, got in, and screeched away after them.

The new car didn't even bother me. There was no time for that now; I was more concerned about finding the missing links of the story and was grateful for what Linda provided. A Lexus, of course! Why hadn't I thought of that? And it was so easy to tail, being the most garish metallic gold color *any* car company makes. I whipped a fast U-turn.

The drive wasn't far. LA is laid out so that the fanciest neighborhoods are often only blocks from the ghettos, and the valley is no exception. I had only to weave a few miles into the hills, which separate the basin and valley, allowing a safe distance between my car and Linda's, though I knew there was nothing to worry about. Her eyes were certainly glued on the truck, which I could also see; its wheels barely shouldering the narrow lanes, which wind through the hills. Both vehicles pulled into the circular drive of a stunning Italianate villa, where

I could see that the view from the house must be magnificent. Somewhere in the story, it would have to be made clear that the house was *exactly* what Patrick had always dreamed of.

Sitting there then, I had a bit of a relapse on my don't-hunt-for-Robert/Randy resolution; I thought there had to be further attempts by Patrick, though I didn't want to overuse the Sony thing; that would seem so much like stalking, wouldn't it? I already felt these visits to Linda had bordered on that—though the reward had now certainly been worth it. But still . . . maybe it could be done in more of a private-eye modus operandi? Or Patrick could be more active, go through the mailbox (Robert/Randy surely wouldn't still be living there), see if there were any clues. Maybe Patrick could bribe the neighbors for info. Robert/Randy would absolutely be cozy with the neighbors, he was probably one of their best customers. But then, there'd be all that messy, low-life stuff, digging through the trash with the trash. I sure didn't want to find myself in some lethal predicament with a crystal freak. I was getting spoiled having it all just *come* to me.

And then it did. The most fortuitous, beautiful thing happened right at that moment while I observed the still-amusing spectacle of Linda and the hapless movers (from a comfortable distance). A matching! Lexus pulled behind Linda's and an impossibly gold-chain-bedazzled and pompadour-toupee-sporting Robert stepped out. He put his hands on his hips and seemed to scan the horizon like a dumbfuck feudal lord surveying his kingdom.

Now I had them by the balls. It was time to begin to prepare for the castration. I was on one of the roller coaster highs; and while I knew there were dips to come, I rode the high. I was still deep into act 2, but there was no harm in anticipating gleefully the eventual outcome of act 3 and the story itself.

—

Ms. Dark's outline for part 2 of act 2 went something like this: The protagonist's reversals continue until he begins to make headway. Then, midway through the act, new information, or the triumph over a major obstacle, turns everything 180 degrees to force the protagonist to face an even greater obstacle than he or the audience had imagined. Now the protagonist is in big trouble, forced to reflect and make a deeper commitment to his mission.

I think it was coming into focus how Patrick has been handling all of this, if not completely clear quite yet. The headway was that he's successfully writing his script, right? Or is it that he's getting closer in his hunt for Lisa and Randy?

or both? Yes, that seems likely. And, definitely, the triumph over the obstacle is that he does locate the two script-stealers; and the outrageous dilemma he now has to face is what the fuck to do.

Anyway, back to the message. Linda said she was sorry she hadn't called; she'd been very busy. She'd moved. She hoped all was well. "Talk to you soon." That sort of thing. Priceless. No mention of the script, no new phone number, no address, really just the royal brush-off. I was happy to have the material. I copied the message down verbatim and, just for the hell of it, called Linda again to get what I knew would be the next scene. The one where Lisa's phone had been disconnected, and there's no forwarding number.

"We're sorry, the number you have dialed is no longer in service. Please check the number and try your call again." I loved that one! I was hoping to get it! See, anything else wouldn't have been as realistic. I immediately jotted the scene down and proceeded to the next.

For a few days, I pondered what was next, scanning the trades for news of the sale, which had most assuredly happened. I was now convinced the damage had been done in the first few days after I'd given the script to Robert. Yes I know; at first I'd thought it unlikely, even impossible. But during these past weeks I'd learned the internet proficiently and discovered through public records hundreds of spec script, treatment, even *idea* sales that had closed instantly. I'd learned I'd been the classic Hollywood peon, in possession of an ignorance so profound it begged to be told in, well, in a story. I jotted the idea down for use another time. This story of a sweet, innocent farm boy who comes to the big city and gets regally fucked had been told countless times before, of course. But not in the way I could tell it. I'd show them.

Sure enough, one day as I was wiping clean the little bistro table in the country-clutter cafe where I now spent many afternoons pounding away at the script, or occasionally, at a short story which came to mind and wouldn't go away, I happened across a *Hollywood Reporter*. It was an issue from many days prior, how had I missed that one? There was a huge photo of Robert, smiling broadly above a bold headline that screamed, RECORD AMOUNT PAID FOR SCRIPT. Below that, a subheading read "First time writer receives $7.8 million and percentages for *Dr. Grim*."

As you've seen, in the new script I'd altered things just slightly so Linda and Robert became Lisa and Randy, and Patrick's ripped-off script became, well, I just reversed everything and titled it **Dr. Grin**—altered slightly from the original title of Patrick's **Dr. Grim**—I felt I'd lose the story if I veered too far. Fuck whatever happened with the copyright problem. That's a joke, isn't it? Unfortunately, I already knew there was a copyright on **Dr. Grin.** I found it on the government website—**and,** for good measure, Robert had copyrighted **Dr. Grim** too. But you can't own a copyright to a title only!

—

After that day, I moved a little slower on the new script. I was sadder, but even **more** driven, more focused. I spent a few days hitting the pavement, visiting entertainment lawyers I'd seen ads for in the trades. Big, splashy graphics proclaiming virtuous intentions. I was under a delusion there was some legal, even ethical recourse.

But every Rolex–and–pinkie-ring-wearing attorney told me the same thing. I was up shit creek without a paddle. Many of them shook their heads; some even expressed disgust, throwing their hands up in the air, admonishing me like a schoolboy for being an insane, half-witted turd. One man, upon hearing the disputed script was the now-famous **Dr. Grim,** first burst out laughing, then threatened to call the police if I, an obvious charlatan, wasn't out of his office in two seconds. I stumbled out of the building near tears and got my jacket caught in the revolving door. Round and round it went, as the door perpetually filled and emptied with a succession of oblivious businesspeople, cell phones sewn to their ears, noses in the air. Nobody offered to help, or even stop the door so I could free it. Finally I stepped out, onto the sidewalk, turned, and watched my now-tattered coat circle a few more times. One woman refused to get into the compartment with it, calmly waiting for the next. I heard her say something into her phone about the homeless problem as I walked on.

I spent a few more afternoons just sitting outside the mansion, watching the comings and goings. Every day there was activity. Workmen of every kind— wallpaper hangers, carpenters, painters, cabinet makers, plumbers, pool guys, gardeners and landscapers, tile setters, interior decorators, and even architects (a forthcoming addition?). I watched as Robert directed them all in a sort of comic silent-movie fashion, since I couldn't hear what was happening. But I could see that he was being the world-class asshole that he was. Frequently, after some animated talk with one of the workmen, Robert would storm inside; and the man would flip him off. I'd get a good laugh and tap away the scene on the computer. Sometimes, Linda would arrive and unload piles of bags and boxes from department stores and boutiques on Rodeo Drive. After several days of this, a woman suddenly appeared from inside as she pulled up. A maid, dressed in a ridiculous stereotypical costume—the stupid clip-on hat, the white apron, the pleated skirt. She helped Linda, who'd apparently had her hair done that day—it was a shocking red—unload the day's shopping bounty; and they both trotted inside.

I'd decided that, for whatever reason, Robert and Linda were living there together. A few futile attempts to tail Robert to wherever else he went led me to the conclusion that except for a couple of steakhouse bars, furniture stores, and the Lexus dealer, he didn't *go* anywhere. After all these years, were these two shacking up? Or better yet, had Linda put some sort of ultimatum into play? involving the theft maybe? a juicy little blackmail? That got me excited for a time, as I imagined the plot twists of such a scenario. But my emotional roller coaster continued as the harsh realities of every day continued.

—

Finally, it all came crashing down; and a debilitating depression set in. A funk so deep it almost lampooned the image of me—alone, completely destitute, even starving at this point. I tried to eat at the missions, quickly learning which one (the one on Las Palmas) had edible food. But, catching my reflection in a greasy mirror one day—in which a gaunt, sallow, hollow-eyed ghost stared back, a tin of swill firmly clasped in his shaking bony fingers, surrounded by a brotherhood of the same—I vowed to die before returning. Instead, I humbled myself at the welfare office, where I received a food stamp debit card from a smug blond who obviously didn't give a fuck. She never once looked at me in the eyes. Not that mine would have met hers anyway. But still. She didn't even try.

So now I had a little food, which I forced myself to eat. Canned beans, tomato soup, Top Ramen—the whole thing was very central casting. But my unemployment benefits had ended, so I didn't have rent money. The landlord, a hideous man in a rancid sleeveless T-shirt permanently stained with what looked like barbeque sauce but could easily have been blood, was knocking twice a day, pounding really. Unshaven, unbathed, unclothed, I sat in my room, with my only friend the laptop, which I refused to hand back to the pawn store, if only temporarily, just so this monster could have *something*. I ignored the poundings, even when they were accompanied by loud and sensational threats. "I'm gonna kill you, motherfucker" was one. And "You make me lose my job asshole you gonna be six feet deep; I know you're in there" was another favorite.

My phone was cut off due to nonpayment. Big deal, right? Weeks had gone by since anybody had called, save for that one bullshit message from Linda. I couldn't remember the last time I'd spoken to my old friends, since I'd started *Dr. Grim*, at least. Now, I was too embarrassed to look them up. Anyway, surely one or two had left town—as they all eventually do—and gone back to their Midwestern family homes to live quiet, fulfilled lives in freshly painted clapboard houses, with scrubbed children and healthy dogs and the Methodist church on Sundays and the PTA on Wednesday nights and all that wonderful banality.

But there wasn't that option for me. My family's home had long since sold; my parents buried years ago. My sister was dead, and Jeff was in the jungle somewhere. There was no getting around it. I was on my own, alone. Stuck.

Soon, I was stuck on the script too.

I had come to the end of act 2 and I knew the final part of the act was *extremely* important. This was where the characters come together. The heart of the story. The moment that ups the ante and makes the audience root for the protagonist's mission even more than before. This is where the moral of the story is hinted at and sometimes where all seems lost. The protagonist may look like he's about to give up. As he faces his biggest hurdles, both the main action line and the subplot seem to be falling apart; it's his darkest hour, his final breaking point, the moment when he realizes all may be lost; and he knows he must deal with that.

But suddenly, something happens. The universe offers him a break. He seizes the moment. He clearly sees what it would mean to accomplish the mission, not just satisfying his pursuit in the story but fulfilling his mission in life as well! By the end of the act, he is standing at the crossroads, poised to take action, his next moves definitive. The climactic turning point approaches. Will he win or lose?

—

Then, early one morning, nearing 4:00 AM, as the rain pounded at my window and seeped in under the warped sill, as I listened to the sounds of a beating in the alley, to a man begging for his life, screaming "Please. Please.

No!" As I heard the popping of a gun, as I stared at my impotent phone, as a car screeched away, as I looked to the pavement, as I saw the bloody body, as my eyes followed the red river into the drain clogged with dead rats and garbage, as my stomach ached and my eyes teared and my body shook— I made the decision. I would enlist the help of Robert to finish the screenplay.

The plan was relatively simple; although things would have to fall perfectly into place, there'd be no room for error. But just in case, I needed a weapon to fall back on. I thought about getting a gun, but aside from the obvious money predicament, I decided it was better not to muddy the waters with one. I'm a writer, after all, and a film buff. Things never go *completely* according to script, and real life is even less certain. No matter how stupid I'd been during all of this, I hadn't lost the capacity to reason. Guns could be traced. There was the whole messy matter of purchase and registration, background checks; and although I was clean, still, a gun was trouble.

But a knife, now that was entirely something else. A great, serrated thing, yes, that would do. Something really menacing looking, something that would make Robert shit in his new silk panties.

The knife was easy. I simply went to my old friend the pawnbroker, leaned over the enormous case of hunting knives and, just as the laptop had beckoned, immediately decided on a stunningly beautiful six-inch blade with a sheath and gleaming mother-of-pearl grip. I paid for it with some of the last cash I had, tucked it under my arm just as I had weeks earlier with the laptop, and proudly strode home. The landlord was waiting on the front stoop this time. Just as the big shithead opened his mouth, I pulled out the knife, very casually, not wanting to be accused of threatening.

"Hi, nice to see you," I said.

The landlord gasped and stepped back.

"What the fuck is that?" he said.

"Oh, this thing?" I said. "Just a little ol' hunting knife."

"You're crazy dude," the landlord said, leaning back to let me through.

I just smiled and walked by, taking two steps at a time once I reached the stairwell.

"Yeah, well, just get me the rent, you hear?" the landlord yelled after, in a tone clearly less ominous than usual. I sensed maybe even a relinquishment of control. Or was I getting too cocky too soon? Maybe. But cocky was better than cowering.

I cleaned myself again then. Things were looking up, and I felt a lot better, like I was getting a move-on. I never saw myself as one for surrendering in the fetal position, some Hollywood cliché, all washed up and drugged out. Even during this bad period, I'd stayed away from serious drink and all drugs, though I *had* been losing it, I admit. But with a shave, a bath, an actual real meal at Cantor's (with the very last of my cash), I was looking good. Well, it was all relative; that was what mattered.

As an afterthought, on the way out the door, I grabbed a minirecorder I used to tape real-life dialogue. Once perpetually in my pocket, as I surreptitiously recorded everything, from the ramblings of the mentally ill on a bus, to the reciting of the daily special by a pompous waiter, the recorder had fallen from my favor since the laptop. Now, thrilled that I'd thought of it, I *knew* it would factor greatly in act 3.

—

By then I had learned Robert and Linda's routine, for the most part. They were so into their new lives I was sure I'd find at least him home any night around nine or ten. Linda had taken to going out with friends, movies and plays, and dinner; I'd tailed her a few times. And Robert? He liked to sit in front of a big freakin' TV screen and watch any moronic shit that was on.

Right before my depression, one evening after I'd seen a security truck among all the workmen's trucks, I'd decided I'd better get a peek inside the house before the alarms, laser sensors, barbed wire, cameras, dogs, or whatever got installed. So I'd stayed all day in my spot down the road until it darkened, when I could sneak into the backyard without being seen. Then, very easily, I slipped around back where the hill sloped and another floor appeared, visible from the rear only. Inside, I could see a tremendous, almost ballroom-sized den, or recreation room or screening room, whatever the rich call their playrooms. (Okay, playroom. Anyway, a screen did fill one wall.) Hiding behind a large rhododendron, I watched as Robert, toupeeless and shirtless, flipped back and forth between Jerry Springer, Cops, and some Asian soft porn, playing with his new digital satellite service.

Just to be sure, I drove by a few more nights. Linda's Lexus was usually gone. (I'd memorized their plates, recently attached, although the difference was only in two letters.) A quick jaunt down the hill always revealed Robert in the same overstuffed La-Z-Boy, stick limbs up over the ottoman, fingers clicking the

remote. Australian crocodile hunters, the **Weather Channel, Nick at Nite**—
the creep watched anything.

Finally, the fence was installed; it was just *there*, though I had been down
the street until 4:00 PM that day, returning only five hours later. How could
that be? Didn't these things have to be set in cement or something? Whatever.
I supposed they could've done that earlier, then all they would have had to do
was dig the holes and set them in. Anyway, since I wasn't sure if climbing them
would set something off, my watching-Robert-watching-TV days were over. The
next day, I sank into the gloom.

—

But it was with confidence that I pulled up to the house now, this night weeks
later. Confidence that Robert would still be there, widening butt in the same
chair, fattened fingers still on the channel changer. Confidence that Linda would
be out with her face-lifted friends trying to pick up boys half their age, luring
them with blow jobs and money, not necessarily in that order. Confidence that I
would finish act 3 from the visit, and, therefore, the utmost confidence that my
predicament was almost over, that my living nightmare was coming to a close,
that the shadow of a man I'd become would soon be a memory, replaced by a
three-dimensional character brimming with substance, a leading man any film
viewer would want to be in the company of.

Linda's car was gone, and Robert's was there. Easy enough. Almost too easy.
As I stepped to the humongous antique Indian temple doors, I wondered—as
I had only on rare occasions through this whole thing—what Robert expected
me to do. Surely, he must have figured that at some time, I would appear. This
had been an egregious act of betrayal, and no matter how spineless or stupid the
victim, such an act would rarely be ignored? Would it? I didn't think Robert was
that stupid. So what was it then?

I rang the bell. I would get the answer soon enough.

Heels clicked closer and closer, and a little hatch opened up. Peering
through the minibars, like through a food drop in solitary, I recognized the maid.
She said something in French.

"Excuse me?" I said.

"May I help you, monsieur," she asked, in a thick accent.

"I'm here to see Robert."

"He eez expecting you, no?"

"Well yes, I think he should be."

"Your name, monsieur?"

"Just tell him the doctor is here."

"Zee doctor?" the nurse said. "There eez something wrong?"

"Yes," I said. "Tell him I need some help."

"I am so sorry. I am, how you say, confused. I will go get monsieur now."

With that, the little hatch snapped shut; and the heels clicked away. I waited, still confident, even more so, that Robert would arrive at the door shortly. I loved my little bit about the doctor. I'll have to remember that, I thought, since I hadn't turned the tape recorder on, and I didn't carry around the pad anymore, always having the laptop, which was snuggled under my arm then too, along with the knife.

The wait was a little longer than I expected, but, by-and-by, there were footsteps again; this time with exaggerated force, as if some fiercely booted but unconvincing man was approaching. I recognized the walk. No amount of leaden footwear could hide that tinny gait. The entire door swung open this time like the entrance to Emerald City, and there he was. The bogus wizard himself. He certainly looked the part; dwarfed by the splendor of the surroundings, he seemed a meek little mouse (or rat), and the pompadour—tilted slightly as if hurriedly fastened—didn't help with the rat thing.

"Peter," Robert said. "I've been expecting you." He stepped back, allowing me into the castle.

"I would imagine so," I said, stepping past him.

The clicking of the maid's heels came from nowhere again.

She was carrying a coat daintily across her arm, and scurried past us, as if we were men at a construction site, harassing her with catcalls.

"Au revoir," she said curtly.

"See you tomorrow," Robert said after her. Then he turned to me. "She's pissed. We had an evening planned . . . if you catch my drift."

"Oh," I said. "So sorry to ruin your plans." Not that Robert hadn't ruined *my plans.*

"Never mind," Robert said. "Obviously, this is important. What took you so long?" He looked at me with a bemused lilt.

"Oh, this and that," I said. "I got held up with a project."

"Really?" he said, shutting the door behind us with a thud, which echoed through the enormous foyer.

I took it in for a second. Some reproduction faux Greek and Roman statuary stuff, a lot of marble, a couple of Persian rugs. Adorning one wall was an enormous landscape of a Tuscany hillside, cherubic nymphs of nebulous sexuality splashing about a pond, that sort of thing. I looked back at Robert, now smirking.

"What sort of project?" he asked, as he gestured toward a room off to the side. We stepped into a banquet-size dining room, with an immense Queen Anne table and at least eighteen gaudy red velvet upholstered chairs.

"Nice, isn't it?" Robert said.

"I like the house; but you have tacky taste," I said. "Let's talk somewhere else."

I was clutching the laptop and knife tightly. He noticed.

"What have you got there?"

"My computer," I replied, hoping I hadn't sounded nervous.

He laughed. "Whatever for?"

We stepped back into the foyer. "Oh, thought we'd work on something," I said.

Robert gave me a twisted smile, which added fuel to his eyes. "Look, punk. I know you think you got a beef with me; maybe you do, a little. We can talk about that. But if you're here to play any fucking games, I'll kick you out of here on your ass."

"Hey, calm down. No games; thought we'd talk is all."

He looked me up and down then paused for a few seconds.

—

"Downstairs," he grunted, pointing to some stairs hidden behind the grander main case. We stepped down without words into the great room I had come to know. From inside, it was still nice, but already the place seemed a pale imitation of what I'd expected to find, or maybe feel. There were no real worthy pieces, nothing rare or truly beautiful, nothing even antique. Just a lot of electronic shit—big screen, stereo components, cameras, some kind of satellite or DVD player, and a lot of other crap. Everything looked absurdly ostentatious, existing only because it appeared to be worth something, or was somebody's idea of what the rich should have. I had seen this before, this type of decorating, when I worked for a Beverly Hills house painter one summer. The rich often have a lot of stuff just for the sake of having stuff. Outrageous pieces of shit, bronze horses, elephants, clay pots and vases, and other meaningless crap just to fill space in their cavernous but, in all other senses of the word, **bankrupt** homes. This was especially so in Hollywood, which had once surprised me. I had imagined, before coming to LA, that everybody's homes were full of literary books and *real* art, with music played live on pianos, and art and foreign films overflowing everybody's personal DVD collections. People went to the symphony or the ballet or theatre. Now I laugh at my ignorance; what had I thought LA was, a Henry James novel? It didn't take long to learn Hollywood was tacky central.

Once downstairs, Robert picked up the familiar remote, and the door to the staircase slammed shut.

"Everything's rigged here," he said. "So don't try anything stupid." He picked up a box of cigarettes and slammed them against a wall (to pack them, I suppose, but what a packing!) Then he withdrew one, putting it to his lips in what seemed to me, along with the punk routine, a newly practiced tough guy persona which only came off as bad acting. Or maybe this is what the newly rich were like, just really I'm-so-holy; but, of course, Robert had always been greasy. Anyway, I had a hard time taking seriously someone who so preposterously weightlifted the top half of his body, and left his legs birdlike. And always wore short pants.

We stepped toward a sitting area, consisting of a large overstuffed couch and two matching chairs, where I plopped myself presumptuously on the sofa. Robert didn't sit.

Though my plan was to get through act 3 then and there, I knew we'd obviously need to discuss the painful *other* matter; so I let Robert instigate that resolution. I reached into my pocket and flipped on the tape player just as he began.

"I was hoping I'd see you soon, get this out of the way," he said, as he stepped to a little minibar in a corner with two 50s modern stools. He picked up ice tongs and dipped into a bucket, then put the ice into two bucket glasses.

"Drink?" he asked. *It was all very Austin Powers*, I thought, *though Robert was likely going for the rat pack.*

"Sure," I said. "Gin, if you have it." I was slightly concerned about the drink, but I'd eaten and didn't want to appear to *not* want alcohol. Maybe things would get really rolling if Robert got drunk.

"Now I know you had like a couple ideas," he was saying. I had to hold my tongue there, as you can imagine. I reached for the drink and took a sip, then watched as Robert took a much longer gulp. *Yes, this would be nice, just like in the movies*, I thought, **letting him get drunk**. But I didn't want it to be too predictable. I wanted an original script.

"With the doctor and all," Robert continued.

"At least a couple," I said, as I fiddled through my pocket to feel the humming of the tape recorder.

"Look, hear me out, it's the best you got," he said, slamming his already finished drink on the glass coffee table, which I now noticed looked remarkably similar to the table in that sitcom **Frasier**'s TV show living room. Those **hideous** squat legs.

"I'll give you ten grand, seeing as how you threw in a few lines," he suddenly said.

We stared at each other like a couple of jungle cats. For a bit I thought Robert might suspect the recorder; it was just too pathetic. Maybe one of those corrupt lawyers had instructed him on this. Maybe the same one who had kicked me out, maybe that **same** asshole called Robert and threatened him with what he knew. With what I had learned about this town, any number of sleazebags could be running this show now. Part of me even **hoped** that one of those lawyers had come to Robert, and skimmed off a large slice of the pie.

But I didn't say anything. Within seconds I softened my glare, folded my hands in my lap, and sat there like a little princess, for Christ's sake. Actually, I was trying to suppress a laugh that would surely come out deranged, and Robert would freak if I sat there in hysterics like a lunatic. So I had to avoid that to keep composure; I couldn't let the cat out of the bag. Yet. But Jesus. It was hard not to crack up at the stupid fuck. Ten thousand lousy dollars when the guy had just cashed a check for seven million!

Robert started to pace, perhaps wondering what the counteroffer would be. Maybe he intended all along to start low, maybe I could've settled for hundreds of thousands of dollars. But by now I wasn't interested. I'd long since crossed the threshold, didn't want to play the game. I had only the one thing, the most important thing, on my mind. I had to have the final act of **Final Draft**. And there was only one way to get it.

"Well, what can I say Robert? It's your show. It has been since I handed you the script." "Look, buddy," he was clearly surprised, even disturbed, by my bizarre insouciance. He snarled, then moved to the bar, where he filled his glass again. This time he skipped the ice. He drank the new drink in one swallow and filled the glass again, again skipping the ice. Then he came to me and stood, very close. Close enough so I could smell his rank breath, see the rotten teeth. (Steroids? Meth? Why hadn't he had those fixed yet? He could certainly afford it now.)

"*Dr. Grim* was *my* invention, you know that," he growled.

So that was it! The name change? Could that have convinced him that the story was, in fact, his? Or had there been other changes significant enough so it might really have been his by the time it was sold? I dismissed the thought instantly. Aside from the impossibility that Robert had the *talent*, I was careful not to regress into a simpering dog.

"Okay then," I said, back to business. "I'll take it."

Robert pulled back, astonished. "What?"

"I said fine." I paused and set the laptop on a glass end table, careful not to reveal the knife inside my jacket. For a second, I wished the knife was smaller, then dismissed that thought too, irritated at myself for all the second-guessing.

"I didn't come here to discuss that anyway," I said, looking for an electrical outlet, as if proceeding with a common activity. I found one and leaned way over to reach it, stretching the cord to its maximum length.

"What are you doing?" Robert asked. I could see that of all the scenarios he had prepared for when he finally met up with me again, this one had not crossed his mind. It pleased me that I could appear so focused—when inside I was a fire raging—that I could portray such control, that very likely I *was* in control.

"I came here for help on my new screenplay, Robert. Since you did such a bang-up job on the doctor, I was hoping you'd help me with the final act. I'm stuck." I said this all very matter-of-factly, avoiding the temptation to be sarcastic. I would play this straight.

"Man, you are fucking crazy. Are you serious?" he said. But he eyed the laptop as he spoke, almost hungrily, readying himself for whatever brainstorming I felt like doing. Then he started to sit, as if this were the most natural thing for the two of us to do together.

"First." I held out my hands, palms up, to stop him. "Write me the check."

Robert stepped back and smiled slyly. "Of course," he said. "But this is still very weird, dude." Here was a man in his fifties calling somebody dude, *great* stuff for the script; everything was falling into place nicely. And I continued to be thrilled about the booze factor, eyeing my drink, still only one sip gone. I hoped he wouldn't notice this. But he'd already had three that I'd seen, plus whatever came before. It wouldn't be long before he was completely incoherent.

"Have another drink," I ventured. "To celebrate."

"Absolutely," he said, dutifully marching, almost skipping to the bar this time. I could see he was feeling victorious, that the situation had ended with a result far easier than he expected. "How's yours? Ready?"

"In a minute," I said, quickly picking up the glass and bringing it to my lips in case he looked, which he didn't.

Robert finished pouring and went to a far corner of the room where a large cherrywood desk sat. I hadn't noticed it during any of my Peeping-Tom visits. Well, why would I have? It's not like he ever sat there. What would he do there? Except maybe write checks out to the peons, which more or less he was doing right then.

I watched as he fumbled through a drawer, found his checkbook, scrounged through another drawer, found a pen, and began to write the check out with a deep sigh. I bit my lip. The ol' emotional roller coaster was climbing and dipping.

"Where does Linda fit in? I thought to ask. I couldn't tell you where that came from. Maybe I was trying to fill the momentary silence, maybe for a second I actually gave a shit, maybe I wondered when she might be coming home, into the room, joining us for a nice, cozy drink.

"Oh, don't worry about her," Robert said. "I'm stringing her along, just keeping her happy for the time being. I'll get rid of her soon enough." A few seconds later he continued, softer. "She's a high-maintenance broad," he said, as if thinking aloud.

"What does that mean?" I asked.

"Whatever you want it to mean. What did she do? Why the fuck should I support her?" he said. He finished scribbling and made his way to me with the check.

"Nothing, I guess," I said, taking it. "Thanks. We're all square then."

I stuffed the check into the pocket where the recorder was. As Robert turned to sit in the familiar La-Z-Boy swivel chair, I felt again for the recorder and flipped it off, pulling my hand out of the pocket just as he turned around.

All of a sudden, things were back full circle. The two of us, old friends, preparing to work together on a script—an idea I was convinced was going to be *the* one. It was almost enough to make a guy teary.

"So tell me about it," Robert said. "What's the hook?"

"Hang on a second, I have a few lines to put in here, then I'm just going to have you read it," I said, quickly typing in the last few scenes, right up to where Patrick quickly types in the last few scenes. This takes just long enough for Robert to get restless and go to the bar for another drink.

I looked up from the keyboard and saw that he seemed to be swaying now, as he reached the bar and poured the gin. He even missed the glass a little. Perfect. By the time he returned and plopped himself in the chair, I'd completed the scene where Randy goes to the bar, pours himself a drink, and misses the glass.

I unplugged the computer then and carried it to Robert. "There's enough time on the battery for you to read it," I said, as he took the laptop.

"I can't believe we're doing this dude," he said, blinking to focus on the little screen. I stepped behind the chair, and Robert tilted his head up as if to say how weird *that* was; but he didn't protest, by then he was a drunken pig.

"I hope it doesn't bother you, reading over your shoulder," I said, feeling for the knife.

"Kinda creepy, this whole thing is," he slurred. "But whatever."

Final Draft

Screenplay by Peter Hansen

Fade In:
1. Int. Los Angeles Apt. Dusk

Credit Sequence: Three people are sitting on a sofa. One, a
man in his early fifties, bald, and grotesquely top-heavy from
bodybuilding, is reading a script. On his left, we see a very thin
woman, also in her early fifties. On his left, we see a younger,
handsome though weathered man, about forty. We pull in to
reveal the title page. We see it reads,

Dr. Grim
A Screenplay by Patrick Johnson

When Robert saw that title, he looked up at me curiously.
"Oh, I just put that in. We'll be changing it," I said.
That seemed to satisfy him, and he settled into reading.

It took him an amazingly long time to realize what was going on. I had slipped the knife out of its sheath effortlessly (but carefully, since we were facing an ornate faux Liberace-framed mirror on a wall not ten feet away) during the *credit* sequence, and was hovering over the clueless Robert for the longest time, waiting for the moment that *had* to come, right? He couldn't be that drunk, could he? But he continued clear into act 2 almost to the part where the caricature French maid opens the door of Randy's mansion to see Patrick standing there with a laptop. Robert had made a few grunting noises, even laughed a few times, nodded his head knowingly a few more times, as if there were characters that reminded him of people he knew or situations he recognized like with any good writing. I made a few animal noises myself, in response, every now and then. I hadn't expected to stand there so long looking over his shoulder like some dumbass. I didn't know what was going through his head, wasn't sure exactly what was going through *my* head; it was beginning to spin. The entire story was being expunged; no . . . more like corkscrewed . . . from me.

But Robert, drunken fuck, finally *did* get it.

There was an awful yet wonderful silence as he literally stopped breathing, and I realized the moment had come. I stepped back a bit in case he swung around sharply, but he simply stopped scrolling on the laptop and looked up. Five minutes must have passed in pre-draw duel mode before he finally spoke.

"You're insane," he said.

"Type that in," I said.

"What?"

"Scroll to the end and continue the story. That's what we're here for," I said. "I'm standing right behind you with the knife. You got to page 79, right? Anyway, I'm standing with the knife poised to enter the back of your neck, though I'd prefer we go with me reaching around and holding it to your throat. Which is better, do you think? After all, you're the editor."

He didn't respond, and he didn't start scrolling. I couldn't tell if he was frozen in fear or trying to grasp, in his boozed state, just what was happening. Then beads of sweat appeared on the back of his neck, and I thought *fear*. Good.

"Okay, so now I am going to bring the tip of this very effective instrument of death to the back of your neck and start digging in until you scroll down, like I said, and type the scene. Exactly as it is happening. Except you'll have to tell me why you are breaking a sweat. I'm thinking you're scared shitless, am I right?"

Robert still didn't respond.

"Okay, so this scene won't have much dialogue from Randy, that's fine. But he *will* type the scene," I said.

Robert's now-shaking hands went to the laptop.

"I wish I hadn't been so dramatic with that 'effective instrument of death thing,' I said. But you have to put it in because I want everything to be authentic." I watched as he struggled to get to the end of the script, still about twenty pages past where he'd read.

"Okay, that's it," I said. Now, see where I've gotten to where Randy, who's pretty drunk, sits down. That's where you pick it up. You have to start where it takes the dumbfuck most of the script to even realize what it's about? Isn't this just brilliant? See, it's a Chinese box, Robert. It's a Chinese box of a story!"

"So . . . what do I put in first?" he said.

"Um . . . how about this:

Scene 116 Int. Randy's Media Room—Night
It takes Randy an amazingly long time before he realizes what is going on. We see Patrick standing behind him, the knife in his hand, poised to plunge it into Randy at the first sign of trouble.

"That's good, isn't it?" I said.

"Uh, yeah."

"Then type it."

Robert made the entry as I read over his shoulder.

"Okay," I said. "Now put in the part where Randy suddenly wakes up and stares out in space for a few minutes and the two of them kind of wait each other out."

He hesitated; and for the first time, I touched the back of his neck with the knife. I made sure I didn't nick the skin though. I don't know why. I guess I was keeping all my options open.

"Do it!" I said.

"Okay . . . what do I put?"

"You know, I do not understand why you need all this help from me. *You* are the talent here." I gave an exaggerated sigh. "Okay, enter this:"

Scene 116 Continued
There was an awful silence as Randy literally stopped breathing, and Patrick realized the moment had come. He stepped back

a bit in case Randy swung around sharply; but Randy simply stopped scrolling on the laptop and looked up. Five minutes seem to pass in pre-draw duel mode before Randy finally spoke.

Randy: You're insane.
Patrick: Type that in.
Randy: What?
Patrick: Scroll to the end and continue the story. That's what we're here for. I'm standing with the knife poised to enter the back of your neck, though I'd prefer we go with me reaching around and holding it to your throat. Which is better, do you think? After all, you're the editor.

Randy continues to sit motionless. The camera moves in on beads of sweat glistening on the back of his neck and face.

Patrick: Okay, so now I'm going to bring this very effective instrument of death to the back of your neck until you scroll down, like I said, and type the scene. Exactly as it is happening. Except you'll have to tell me why you are breaking a sweat. I'm thinking you're scared shitless, am I right?

Randy continues to sit motionless.

Patrick: Okay, so this scene won't have much dialogue, that's fine. But he *will* type the scene.

The camera moves in on Randy's trembling hands, as they go to the keyboard.

Patrick: I wish I hadn't been so dramatic with that "effective instrument of death" thing. But you have to put it in because I want everything to be authentic.

The camera moves in on Patrick, who we see carefully watching Randy.

Patrick: Okay, that's it. Now, see where I've gotten to where he's pretty drunk, and sits down. That's where you pick it up. You have to start where it takes the dumbfuck most of the script to even realize what it's about? Isn't this just brilliant? See, it's a Chinese box, Randy. It's a Chinese box of a story.

This went on until Robert had completed the scene. It was all going perfectly to plan, except for the final scene; but I wasn't worried, I knew it would come.

And then it did.

—

In the quick flash of a second, I let my guard down. So involved in the script, so focused on Robert's hands on the keyboard, on the words as they appeared on the screen, I hadn't noticed Linda glide the sliding glass door open behind us.

"Drop the knife," her unmistakable voice said.

I felt my heart jump into my throat, not out of fear, but from a sudden impossible, almost euphoric, excitement; so much so, I was afraid I might give away my elation, and the scene would be ruined. I suppressed a smile and looked up slowly into the mirror to see first Robert and me, then Linda, behind us, waving a gun. Then I became slightly disappointed, because she looked so comical standing there, and I'd hoped the story would end on a more serious note. But hey, I would use the cards that were dealt.

She wore stiletto heels and fishnet stockings, and featured another preposterous new hairdo, as if she was going for the twenties flapper look. She'd had something done to her, probably another face-lift, which gave her a deer-in-the-headlights look, exaggerated by the situation she now found herself in. She might have had a boob job too; that was hard to tell since she had them strapped in some sort of bondage-Gautier number, which made her look like an anorexic Pamela Sue Anderson crossed with the Princess Warrior.

But she did have that gun, and I was grateful for that. I'd fleetingly wished, during the standoff with Robert, that I'd chosen a gun, if only because there was a chance things were going to get bloody and I hadn't wanted to do a gore story. I think there is too much violence in the movies, don't you agree? But a gun, well, a gun could bring things to a relatively tidy ending. Maybe things would end with somebody shot, but with a good chance of a cleaner finish, maybe one hole through the heart or chest; and you wouldn't even need to show that on the screen. You could do it like in the old days, where the dying man (or woman, we'd see soon enough) simply fell to the floor, a hand over the wound, things more implied than visual.

"C'mon, Peter," Linda said. "I mean it; I'm not kidding."

I instinctively drew the knife to Robert's throat instead.

"Jesus, Linda, he's crazy!" Robert yelled.

"Well, we thought something like this might happen . . . didn't we?" she said.

"Not like this, I didn't," Robert said.

"Oh, I always knew he was a little off his rocker," Linda said.

"Hey, you two just go on like I'm not even here," I said, *very* glad Linda had just said rocker, because it gave me an important idea involving the La-Z-Boy. I pressed the knife to his throat with a chokehold.

Robert, drenched in sweat, began to cry.

"Jesus! How am I supposed to use this?" I said. "I want this to be good! Now I've got some sniveling steroid head and Mae West meets Nicole Ritchie with a gun. I don't want to be doing a comedy, for God's sake! Is that even a real fucking gun?"

"Yes," Linda said. "And what do you mean Nicole Ritchie?" She got a stupid look on her face as if she might have just been flattered.

"No," Robert said between tears, "he doesn't mean you look thirty, you dipshit. He means you look like you could use a good meal."

Linda looked hurt, then quickly got back to business. "Well, screw you too."

"Linda, you have to shoot him," Robert said.

"What are you, some kind of idiot?" I said. "Can't you see I'm going to slice your throat from ear to ear?"

"I don't think you're going to do that," he said. He suddenly stopped crying and seemed to have grasped something.

"It's not the story you want," he continued.

"How do you know what I want?"

"You want the protagonist to achieve his mission; you want the perfect act 3," he said. "That won't happen if you kill me."

He paused and took a couple of very deep breaths. "Because you'll go to prison for murder. True, the antagonist, or one of them anyway, will be dead;

but there will be no resolution . . . the audience will be left unsatisfied; they will feel cheated. And all your work will have been for shit."

"Well, how do you propose we end it?" I said, still pressing the knife close to his throat. He appeared less nervous with each minute, as he attempted to talk his way out. I knew that a good act 3 contained the crisis, the climax, and the story's resolution. I knew Robert was telling the truth, that in order for my story to be perfect, I needed a scene or sequence of scenes in which the final outcome of the story is determined by the protagonist's actions.

"I don't know what you're going to do buddy," Robert said. "But you ain't got shit if you cut me up. All you got is another stupid slasher pic."

"I think you're both crazy now," said Linda, waving the gun again, as if everybody forgot she had it.

"Shut up, Linda," Robert said.

"So go on, give me a better final act then," I said.

"I think Linda should shoot your ass. Then you'd be like a martyr, you know?"

"Now you're the crazy one," I said. "You think I came all this way to die and let you two go free with *two* scripts?"

"I think you came all this way for the perfect story. I don't think it matters whether you live or die," Robert said.

"Well, I'm not gonna have the perfect story if *I* die, asshole. The *bad* guy has to die."

"But you *are* the bad guy." Robert said.

"How do you figure that?"

"Because you're the murderous lunatic with the knife."

"That's a revenge thing."

"Revenge is different than justice."

"What the fuck does that mean?"

"If Randy is going to die, it has to be some divine act. It's too pat for you to do it."

"Who the hell is Randy? What is going on here? You guys are both loony," Linda said. I could see in the mirror that she was picking lint off her dress. After a second, she looked up dumbly. "What do you mean two scripts? Robert? Are you not telling me something?"

"Shut the fuck up, Linda."

"You quit using that language with me; I am really starting to get irritated here. Who's the one with the gun anyway?"

I was losing patience. I could see them mind fucking me. The two of them, me, this ridiculous house, surrounded by all this crap. I was starting to go a little batty, maybe I was crazy; I was starting to spin, or maybe it was the swivel chair. I was leaning on it too hard; it had started to move of its own accord; it forced the knife into Robert's flesh a little deeper; the knife was making a dent in his skin now; we could all see what was happening in the mirror; it was happening fast.

"Shoot him, quick!" Robert yelled. "He's gonna kill me."

But within that fraction of a second I swung the chair to continue its rotation so that the chair, Robert sitting in it, faced Linda just as she pulled the trigger. I ducked behind, and Robert caught the bullet with a thud, a louder thud than I would've thought. Like a fist hitting a punching bag.

"Just the one bullet," I yelled. "No more." And Linda dropped the gun, performed her scene impeccably. There would be no need for a second take.

She stood there now, mouth agape, as if waiting for further instructions.

Robert lay convincingly dead, though maybe there was *some* question, since it had been *amazingly* clean. So I felt for a pulse on the very neck the knife had rested against seconds earlier. No pulse. I looked at the wound, a perfect circle, without color but black as space at the same time. Robert dribbled a little red spit from his mouth, but otherwise, it was nearly a bloodless death.

Then I scanned his throat and neck for any abrasions the knife might have made but there were none. I reached over the body, to the still-flickering computer, right-clicked on the file, and hit the eraser software icon I'd installed a few weeks prior. (I'd learned deleting a file doesn't really delete it forever.) A screen appeared asking whether I was sure I wanted to erase the file named **Final Draft**. I positioned the cursor over YES and hit it several times. Erasing a file with the software is really just overwriting it so I wanted to be sure. I left the laptop, went to the desk, and calmly wiped the knife clean, put it back in its sheath, and placed it in a drawer next to a stapler and some paperclips. Then I picked up the phone and dialed 911.

Linda had sunk to the floor, sobbing uncontrollably and muttering how her life was ruined, and she'd just had all this work done. She lifted her head as I spoke to the police, then she fell back to the floor and wailed.

I had reached the climax, the end of the crisis, where all act 3s must eventually arrive. This is where the protagonist has finally destroyed the bad guys. Now the story was complete but for one more thing: The resolution.

Epilogue

So I got my Final Draft. Sure, I had to erase it, but it's still there where it counts, in my head. I'll pull it up again someday. Meanwhile, I had to get through the trial where, of course, Linda tried to accuse me of planning and killing Robert due to the script theft, which she admitted, hoping my *obvious* motive would clear her. She told the court she'd tried to help him because I'd held a knife on him, when the chair swiveled like that. She wasn't good with a gun; she missed, and it was all an accident . . . blah, blah. Right. That's when I pulled out the tape where Robert said he was going to ditch her and where I said to Robert I was perfectly fine with the ten grand, when we'd made our weepy peace and decided to work on another project together. As for the knife, I said I didn't know what she was talking about; and since there weren't any wounds on Robert or fingerprints on the knife (obviously just an *objet d' art* of Robert's) her attorney couldn't do anything with that worthless evidence.

And the laptop? There was nothing of interest on the hard drive.

Needless to say, the jury saw it all fairly; and Linda was convicted of first-degree murder with a life sentence, with a chance of parole after twenty-five years. Meantime, her court confession that they'd stolen **Dr. Grim** gave me the ammunition to hire a good lawyer to take the case, which we won, giving me most of Robert's estate (including the house) in a civil suit.

Now I'm writing this script called **The Dream Reader** about a guy who gets all these great story and script ideas from dreams.

—

Thanks to all of the teachers and writers who guided me. Please note that this story includes passages, quotes and near-quotes from numerous scriptwriting textbooks and guides, taken from notes I scribbled during years of writing workshops. I've done my best to include them only in relevant classroom or learning scenes. My apologies that I wasn't more diligent back then, in documenting the titles of the textbooks.

www.ingramcontent.com/pod-product-compliance
Lightning Source LLC
Chambersburg PA
CBHW031326290526
45784CB00014B/2242